P9-BYB-472

# ADVANCED WOODWORKING

*Other Publications:*

LIBRARY OF HEALTH
CLASSICS OF THE OLD WEST
THE EPIC OF FLIGHT
THE GOOD COOK
THE SEAFARERS
THE ENCYCLOPEDIA OF COLLECTIBLES
THE GREAT CITIES
WORLD WAR II
THE WORLD'S WILD PLACES
THE TIME-LIFE LIBRARY OF BOATING
HUMAN BEHAVIOR
THE ART OF SEWING
THE OLD WEST
THE EMERGENCE OF MAN
THE AMERICAN WILDERNESS
THE TIME-LIFE ENCYCLOPEDIA OF GARDENING
LIFE LIBRARY OF PHOTOGRAPHY
THIS FABULOUS CENTURY
FOODS OF THE WORLD
TIME-LIFE LIBRARY OF AMERICA
TIME-LIFE LIBRARY OF ART
GREAT AGES OF MAN
LIFE SCIENCE LIBRARY
THE LIFE HISTORY OF THE UNITED STATES
TIME READING PROGRAM
LIFE NATURE LIBRARY
LIFE WORLD LIBRARY
FAMILY LIBRARY:
    HOW THINGS WORK IN YOUR HOME
    THE TIME-LIFE BOOK OF THE FAMILY CAR
    THE TIME-LIFE FAMILY LEGAL GUIDE
    THE TIME-LIFE BOOK OF FAMILY FINANCE

HOME REPAIR
AND IMPROVEMENT

# ADVANCED WOODWORKING

BY THE EDITORS OF
TIME-LIFE BOOKS

TIME-LIFE BOOKS
ALEXANDRIA, VIRGINIA

Time-Life Books Inc.
is a wholly owned subsidiary of
**TIME INCORPORATED**

Founder  Henry R. Luce 1898-1967

Editor-in-Chief  Henry Anatole Grunwald
President  J. Richard Munro
Chairman of the Board  Ralph P. Davidson
Executive Vice President  Clifford J. Grum
Chairman, Executive Committee  James R. Shepley
Editorial Director  Ralph Graves
Group Vice President, Books  Joan D. Manley
Vice Chairman  Arthur Temple

**TIME-LIFE BOOKS INC.**

Managing Editor  Jerry Korn
Executive Editor  David Maness
Assistant Managing Editors  Dale M. Brown (planning), George Constable, Thomas H. Flaherty Jr. (acting), Martin Mann, John Paul Porter
Art Director  Tom Suzuki
Chief of Research  David L. Harrison
Director of Photography  Robert G. Mason
Assistant Art Director  Arnold C. Holeywell
Assistant Chief of Research  Carolyn L. Sackett
Assistant Director of Photography  Dolores A. Littles

Chairman  John D. McSweeney
President  Carl G. Jaeger
Executive Vice Presidents  John Steven Maxwell, David J. Walsh
Vice Presidents  George Artandi (comptroller); Stephen L. Bair (legal counsel); Peter G. Barnes; Nicholas Benton (public relations); John L. Canova; Beatrice T. Dobie (personnel); Carol Flaumenhaft (consumer affairs); James L. Mercer (Europe/South Pacific); Herbert Sorkin (production); Paul R. Stewart (marketing)

**HOME REPAIR AND IMPROVEMENT**

Editorial Staff for Advanced Woodworking

Editor  Robert M. Jones
Assistant Editors  Betsy Frankel, Brooke Stoddard
Designer  Edward Frank
Picture Editor  Adrian Allen
Text Editors  Robert A. Doyle (senior), Lynn R. Addison, Peter Pocock
Staff Writers  Patricia C. Bangs, Jan Leslie Cook, Carol J. Corner, Rachel Cox, Steven J. Forbis, Kathleen M. Kiely, Victoria W. Monks, Kirk Young Saunders, Ania Savage, Mary-Sherman Willis
Researcher  Kimberly K. Lewis
Art Associates  George Bell, Fred Holz, Lorraine D. Rivard, Peter C. Simmons
Editorial Assistant  Susan Larson

Editorial Production

Production Editor  Douglas B. Graham
Operations Manager  Gennaro C. Esposito, Gordon E. Buck (assistant)
Assistant Production Editor  Feliciano Madrid
Quality Control  Robert L. Young (director), James J. Cox (assistant), Daniel J. McSweeney, Michael G. Wight (associates)
Art Coordinator  Anne B. Landry
Copy Staff  Susan B. Galloway (chief), Diane Ullius Jarrett, Celia Beattie
Picture Department  Betsy Donahue

Correspondents: Elisabeth Kraemer (Bonn); Margot Hapgood, Dorothy Bacon, Lesley Coleman (London); Susan Jonas, Lucy T. Voulgaris (New York); Maria Vincenza Aloisi, Josephine du Brusle (Paris); Ann Natanson (Rome). Valuable assistance was also provided by: Carolyn Montserrat (Barcelona); Judy Aspinall, Karin B. Pearce (London); Miriam Hsia, Christina Lieberman (New York); Mimi Murphy (Rome).

THE CONSULTANTS: Roswell W. Ard is a consulting structural engineer and a professional home inspector in northern Michigan. He has written professionally on the structural uses of wood and on wood-frame construction techniques, and is experienced in finish carpentry.

Peter Danko, a designer-craftsman in Alexandria, Virginia, specializes in commissioned woodworking. A chair of his design received a Daphne Award from the American Hardwood Institute and is included in the Design Study Collection of the Museum of Modern Art in New York City.

Lawrence R. England Jr. works in L. R. England and Sons, the family cabinetmaking and woodworking business established by his grandfather in Boston in 1900. The firm specializes in the design and construction of custom-made furniture.

Harris Mitchell, special consultant for Canada, has worked in the field of home repair and improvement for more than two decades. He is Homes editor of *Today* magazine and author of a syndicated newspaper column, "You Wanted to Know," as well as a number of books on home improvement.

Stanley N. Wellborn, the Washington, D.C., correspondent for *Fine Woodworking* magazine, has written many articles on woodworking and woodworkers. An avid hobbyist, Wellborn specializes in woodturning and lathe work, particularly faceplate turning.

For information about any Time-Life book, please write:
Reader Information
Time-Life Books
541 North Fairbanks Court
Chicago, Illinois 60611

Library of Congress Cataloguing in Publication Data
Time-Life Books.
Advanced woodworking.
  (Home repair and improvement; 27)
  Includes index.
  1. Woodwork.  I. Time-Life Books.  II. Series.
TT180.A2    684'.08    81-1310
ISBN 0-8094-3480-6    AACR2
ISBN 0-8094-3479-2 (lib. bdg.)
ISBN 0-8094-3478-4 (retail ed.)

© 1981 Time-Life Books Inc. All rights reserved.
No part of this book may be reproduced in any form or by any electronic or mechanical means, including information storage and retrieval devices or systems, without prior written permission from the publisher, except that brief passages may be quoted for reviews.
First printing.
Published simultaneously in Canada.
School and library distribution by Silver Burdett Company, Morristown, New Jersey.

TIME-LIFE is a trademark of Time Incorporated U.S.A.

# Contents

# 1 Rough Wood to Smooth Boards

**Getting off to a good start.** With bench dogs holding a rough-cut board steady and in place, a jack plane shaves thick curls of wood from the high spots, gradually bringing the board down to the flat, mirror-smooth finish needed for fine woodworking. The power-tool equivalent of the hand plane, useful for smoothing quantities of long boards, is the jointer-planer shown in the background. Its circular cutting head makes short work of planing surfaces and squaring edges.

For the woodworker who gazes at a tree and envisions a table within its trunk, or who examines rough boards and sees a paneled wall, design must temporarily take second place to the preparation of the stock. Nature does not provide for tables and panels to spring full-blown from the trunks of trees or the surfaces of boards. Much work must be done on the raw material before it is suitable for woodworking. The lumber must be cut to the needed size, smoothed to a silky finish and then dimensioned to fit the project at hand.

Lumberyards take care of some of these tasks, cutting lumber to stock sizes and custom-cutting it to various specifications. But the scarcity and high cost of the hardwoods used in fine woodworking make a search for alternative sources appealing. In fact, some of the best wood used by professional woodworkers is not purchased at lumberyards at all. It is discovered by reading ads in specialty magazines, which may offer a cache of seasoned cherry or a barnful of old oak siding. Or it is found by checking notices of estate sales of country properties, which often advertise stores of wood along with the furnishing of homes and farms. Farmers themselves, in the course of clearing land, may fill their sheds with good maple or hickory logs and then offer them for sale. And it sometimes is possible to salvage beautiful cabinetry wood from storm-felled trees found in a nearby park or in a neighbor's yard—free for the asking if you will arrange to carry it away.

Transforming this raw wood into boards with straight, parallel faces is the first step in the process of acquiring workable stock. Taking time to do this step carefully not only will result in a precisely dimensioned board that will ensure smooth joints and easy assembly, but will also disclose valuable information on the nature of the wood—how it grew, how it will respond to shaping, how it can be manipulated. Learning to anticipate how growth patterns and grain figurings will react to milling is in fact one of the keys to fine craftsmanship. In Scandinavian countries, woodworkers serving their apprenticeships spend up to five years learning to prepare stock and to understand the character of wood before they are allowed to participate in the actual fabrication of a piece.

Just as it is possible for the connoisseur of fine furniture or joinery to appreciate superior workmanship without ever picking up a tool, so it is possible, of course, for a woodworker to love a piece of wood without ever having laid eyes on the original tree. But the process of preparing the wood from scratch, of converting a bark-covered log into smooth boards, can only deepen the woodworker's knowledge and understanding of this unpredictable material—and his pleasure in creating the ultimate design.

# Understanding Wood

Wood, one of the world's most commonplace natural resources, is also one of the most mysterious. Beautiful to look at and satisfying to work, wood often seems to have a life of its own. For one thing, it has a disconcerting tendency to continue to react to the atmosphere long after it has been cut, surfaced and finished.

Fortunately, it is well within the power of the woodworker to control and manipulate this tendency, and doing so is one of the charms of the craft. By understanding how wood grows and what happens to it as it dries, the woodworker can anticipate and influence its behavior. He can, for example, preshrink the wood by seasoning it, modify the design of the piece to allow for potential shrinking and swelling, or finish the piece to control its response to the environment.

The most commonly used terms in describing wood probably are "hardwood" and "softwood." Although technically they describe the strength of wood, in practice they are simply the lumber industry's handy labels for distinguishing between wood from deciduous trees and that from conifers, or evergreens. Hardwoods, the kind most often used for fine woodworking, come from deciduous trees, and are indeed generally hard, while softwoods are generally soft. But the wood of some deciduous trees, such as basswood, is actually soft, while the wood of some conifers, such as southern yellow pine, is hard.

The characteristics of wood are also determined by the structure of the tree; certain qualities are associated with certain parts. Heartwood, the older wood at the center of the trunk, is often valued for its moisture resistance, for example, while the younger sapwood is more responsive to moisture variations.

How the tree grows also determines the figuring of the wood—the natural coloring patterns and texture of the grain. Grain coarseness or fineness, usually associated with appearance, to some extent also affects the way the wood will finish. Coarse-grained woods, such as oak and walnut, have large, open cells, which when cut produce a slightly pitted surface. Fine-grained woods, such as maple and birch, have small, thick-walled cells, which produce a smooth surface.

The pattern of the grain on a milled board is largely a reflection of the annual growth rings, but it can be emphasized or softened by the manner in which the log is cut. When wood is sliced across the rings at a sharp angle, as in quartersawing (page 10), its graining, or figure, will be linear. On the other hand, plain-sawing (page 10), in which the cuts are roughly parallel to the concentric rings, tends to provide an arced grain.

After the primary conversion from log to rough-cut board, the wood must be seasoned, or dried, until its moisture content is in the correct range (page 12). At this stage many problems can occur that affect the behavior of wood when it reaches the woodworker's hands. Improper drying can result in warping (page 13), checking (page 10) or case hardening. In case hardening, the outside of the wood dries more rapidly than the inside, and interior splitting called honeycombing occurs. There are two good ways to avoid these potential problems: Buy kiln-dried lumber, or air-dry green lumber at home under carefully controlled conditions (page 12).

When you buy wood, whether green or kiln-dried, remember that lumber is graded according to clarity, or freedom from blemishes. Where appearance does not count, you can often save money by using lower grades if you know what to expect of them. Boards in the top grades, First and Second, are required to be 80 to 90 per cent clear of knots and blemishes on both faces and are never less than 6 inches wide and 8 feet long. In the next grade, Select, the boards must be 80 per cent clear on one face and are never less than 4 inches wide and 6 feet long. The grade most frequently used, No. 1 Common, contains about 65 per cent of clear wood on one face and is considered the best all-purpose wood in terms of both yield and price.

In grading, the percentages refer to the maximum number of allowable blemishes. Hardwood grades are based on the poorer of the two faces; softwood grades are based on the better of the two faces.

## Safety Rules for Power Tools

Power tools have greatly extended the ability of the woodworker to shape wood accurately, but they must be treated with the respect due any potentially dangerous piece of machinery. In addition to following the specific safety rules for individual power tools, observe these general precautions:

☐ Never operate a power tool when you are tired or ill or have been drinking alcoholic beverages or taking medicine.
☐ Keep the work area and tool surface uncluttered and well lighted.

☐ Keep the tool clean and lubricated, the blade sharp; check the electrical cord and plug frequently for fraying, nicks or other damage. Make sure the outlet and plug are properly grounded.
☐ Always unplug the tool before making any adjustments.
☐ Do not wear clothing or jewelry that could catch in moving parts. Keep shirt sleeves buttoned or rolled up.
☐ Wear safety glasses and, if the operation is dusty, a dust mask.
☐ Never mark the wood for a saw cut

after the motor has been started.
☐ Feed wood carefully into the blade; never force it to move at a faster rate than the tool can easily accommodate.
☐ Whenever possible, use the safety aids, such as blade guards, provided with the tool. Be especially cautious operating the tool when safety devices must be removed.
☐ Keep children and pets away from the work area.
☐ Do not let your mind wander; concentrate on what you are doing.

## Flaws in the Log That Affect the Lumber

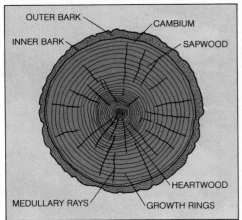

OUTER BARK · CAMBIUM · INNER BARK · SAPWOOD · HEARTWOOD · GROWTH RINGS · MEDULLARY RAYS

**Anatomy of an average tree.** The usable wood in the trunk of a tree lies beneath a protective layer of outer bark and two thin layers of life-supporting tissue. One of these thin layers, the inner bark, carries food from the leaves to the rest of the tree. The other, the cell-producing cambium, is where the cell growth for both the wood and the bark takes place.

The first layer of usable wood, nearest the cambium, is the light-colored sapwood, which carries sap from the roots to the leaves—a function that accounts for sapwood's receptiveness to moisture. The heartwood, beneath the sapwood, is denser and darker and generally more durable; it contains resins, for instance, that make it more resistant to rot. Each of the concentric growth rings represents one year of life, and each is composed of a layer of light springwood and one of darker summerwood, reflecting the two seasons of growth. A high proportion of summerwood to springwood results in a richer, darker-colored wood. Radiating from the center are the medullary rays, which carry food laterally and in some kinds of wood produce a pronounced pattern in the milled lumber.

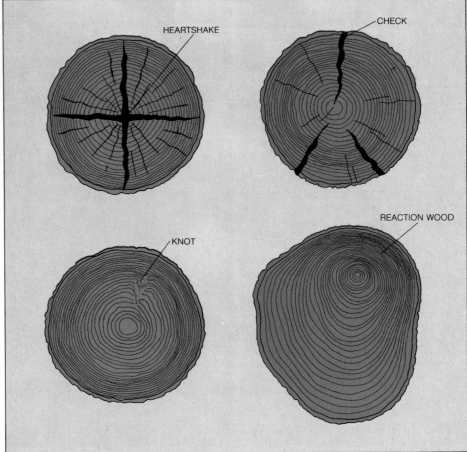

HEARTSHAKE · CHECK · KNOT · REACTION WOOD

**A record of assaults.** Most wood is subjected at some point in its life to conditions that alter its normal development and leave behind defects and injuries. Heartshake, a result of decay or stress, forces the tree to crack at the center and to split along the medullary rays. Checks, which generally are less severe, appear as splits or cracks after the tree is felled; they are caused by separation of the wood fibers along the grain and across the annual growth rings as a result of uneven shrinking. Knots are the ends of broken limbs that have become encased by new growth. Reaction wood, identifiable by its off-center pattern of growth rings, is found in trees that lean sideways because of high winds or a one-directional light source.

# Characteristics Created during the Milling Process

**Variations in milling techniques.** In plain-sawing *(near right)*, the simplest and most common method, the log is sliced lengthwise, or tangentially, into parallel slabs of uniform thickness. This method leaves very little waste, but the boards warp as they dry. In quartersawing *(far right)*, the log is cut into quarters, then into slabs. Shown clockwise from lower left are four cutting patterns: a true radial; a modified radial, in which only the center board runs to the heart; alternating tangential cuts; and a combination of radial and tangential cuts. The true radial is the most desirable. It produces more waste, but it exposes a more attractive grain and yields boards less likely to warp.

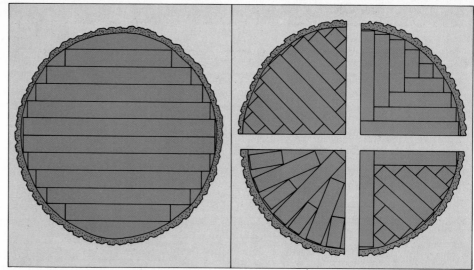

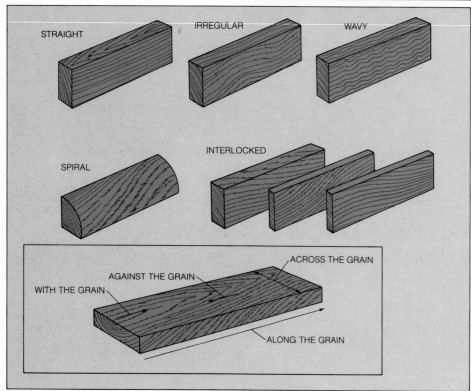

STRAIGHT     IRREGULAR     WAVY

SPIRAL     INTERLOCKED

WITH THE GRAIN   AGAINST THE GRAIN   ACROSS THE GRAIN   ALONG THE GRAIN

**Identifying grain types.** Of the five naturally occurring types of grain, straight grain—found in such woods as ash and oak—has the greatest overall strength but produces the least interesting pattern when sawed. Irregular grain is straight grain that has been deflected from its course by a defect, such as a knot; it can be present in almost any wood. Wavy grain is less strong than straight grain but produces attractive patterns; it is found typically in European walnut and sometimes in hickory. Spiral grain, often found in chestnut, is grain that follows a corkscrew course up the trunk of the tree, producing diagonal patterns when sawed. Interlocked grain, shown here with several slices taken from one block

of wood to expose its change of direction, follows one course and then another. This erratic grain pattern is commonly found in hardwoods such as mahogany and rosewood.

In addition to forming distinctive patterns, grain also moves in a specific direction, reflecting the tree's upward growth. To find the grain direction on a board, run your hand over its surface, first one way, then the other *(inset)*. When you are following the grain, the board will feel smooth; against the grain, the board will feel rough. You can also determine grain direction by examining the grain on the edge of the board—it always slants in the direction of the grain.

**Recognizing defects.** In the milling process, abnormal growth reappears in the form of defects that may weaken the wood. Checks *(above, top)* show up as deep cracks in the end of the board or as surface splits; they tend to worsen as the board shrinks and swells. Knots *(above, middle)* appear as dark whorls, varying in size from pin knots, less than ½ inch across, to knots more than 1½ inches in diameter. If the knot is encased in dead bark, it may eventually loosen and fall out. Reaction wood *(above, bottom)*, with its compressed rings, shows up as a dark streak in the grain pattern of the board; the tension of the rings may cause the board to be brittle and to shrink unevenly.

# A Guide to the Classic Hardwoods

| Material | Characteristics |
|---|---|
| Ash | Coarse to medium-fine texture; good strength, excellent bending qualities; fair workability (prone to distortion); fair with nails, screws, glue; excellent finishing qualities; commonly used for furniture, interior joinery, turning. |
| Beech | Fine, even texture; excellent strength and bending qualities; fair workability (tends to bind when sawed and drilled); fair with nails, screws, good with glue; good finishing qualities; commonly used for furniture, interior joinery, turning. |
| Birch | Fine to medium texture; good strength and bending qualities; good workability; good with nails, screws, glue; excellent finishing qualities; commonly used for furniture, veneer, interior joinery, turning. |
| Cherry | Fine, even texture; good strength and bending qualities; very good workability; good with nails, screws, glue; excellent finishing qualities; commonly used for furniture, veneer, cabinetry, interior joinery, turning. |
| Chestnut | Coarse texture; fair strength, good bending qualities; good workability (tends to bind when sawed); good with nails, screws, glue; excellent finishing qualities; commonly used for furniture, turning. |
| Hickory | Coarse texture; very good strength, good bending qualities; fair workability (tends to dull blades); difficult with nails, screws, good with glue; fair finishing qualities; commonly used for tool handles, sports equipment. |
| Mahogany | Mainly fine, even texture; good strength and bending qualities; good workability (tends to scuff during planing); fair with nails, good with screws and glue; excellent finishing qualities; commonly used for interior joinery, paneling, veneer, cabinetry, turning. |
| Maple | Fine texture; very good strength, good bending qualities; good workability; good with nails and screws, fair with glue; good finishing qualities; commonly used for furniture, veneer, turning. |
| Oak | Coarse but even texture; excellent strength, good bending qualities; good workability; good with nails, screws, glue; good finishing qualities; commonly used for furniture, veneer, interior joinery. |
| Rosewood | From coarse to very fine, even texture; very good strength, good bending qualities; difficult to work (tends to dull blades); poor with nails, good with screws, fair with glue; excellent finishing qualities; commonly used for furniture, veneer, interior joinery, carving. |
| Sycamore | Smooth texture; very good strength, good bending qualities; fair workability; fair with nails and screws, good with glue; excellent finishing qualities; commonly used for furniture, interior joinery, veneer, turning. |
| Teak | Coarse texture; good strength and bending qualities; fair workability (tends to dull tools; power tools tend to burn the surface); fair with nails, screws, glue; fair finishing qualities; commonly used for furniture, veneer, interior and exterior joinery, turning. |
| Walnut | Fine texture; excellent strength, good bending qualities; good workability; good with nails, screws, glue; excellent finishing qualities; commonly used for furniture, veneer, interior joinery, carving, turning. |

**Rating woodworking properties.** When logs are converted into lumber, the wood acquires characteristics that affect its use and handling. The chart at left lists 13 hardwoods commonly chosen for woodworking projects and describes how they look and behave. Also included is a sampling of their traditional uses. Softwoods are not included in the list, since they are used less frequently in woodworking than hardwoods are. The term "texture" here applies to the appearance of the grain, not to its tactile qualities. "Strength" and "bending qualities" refer to ability to withstand impact and to bend without splitting. "Workability" describes how the wood responds to tooling. Each wood is also rated for its ability to hold fasteners and glue and to take finishes, such as stain or paint.

# The Significance of Seasoning

When a living tree is cut, more than half its weight may be water. This water is contained in the cell cavities and cell walls as free water and bound water. When the tree dies, the free water is the first to drain away or evaporate, at which stage the wood is said to be at the fiber-saturation point. In most woods the fiber-saturation point occurs when approximately 30 percent of the wood's weight is water—that is, when its moisture content is 30 per cent.

It is not until the moisture content falls below this fiber-saturation point that the wood begins to shrink. When the moisture content has dropped to 15 per cent, the wood will have shrunk to half its total potential shrinkage. This is not enough to prevent the wood from shrinking after it has been worked, so it must continue to dry until the moisture content of the wood is in balance with the moisture content of the atmosphere. It is then said to have reached an equilibrium moisture content, and it is considered seasoned and ready to be worked.

The fastest way to season wood is to kiln-dry it. In kiln-drying, the lumber is placed in huge ovens, where steam is used to keep the humidity high while the temperature is kept low. Gradually the temperature is raised and the humidity is lowered until the moisture content of the wood has been brought down to the desired level. Air-drying, a slower process, is usually started outdoors and completed indoors. It takes patience and vigilance. Temperature, humidity and air circulation must be controlled so that the wood dries fast enough to prevent decay but slowly enough to prevent checking.

To air-dry wood, begin by marking each board with a number and the date on which the drying is begun. Then stack the wood outdoors, out of the sun and protected from direct rainfall. (If you must dry it indoors, cover it with plastic sheeting to prevent it from drying too rapidly, and check it frequently for fungus; if fungus appears, increase air circulation by loosening or removing the plastic and restacking the lumber.)

Keep the boards off the ground, and separate the layers with sticker strips—lengths of 1-by-2 wood placed 18 inches apart along the length of the stack and aligned vertically from layer to layer. Place boards of uniform length in each stack; overhanging boards will dry too rapidly and warp.

Because end grain dries almost 12 times as fast as side grain, coat the ends of the boards generously with paraffin, white glue, aluminum paint or polyurethane varnish to prevent them from splitting. If the wood is wet, give the ends a preliminary coat of latex paint.

During drying, monitor the moisture content by selecting a board from inside the stack and weighing it periodically. A large piece can be weighed on a bathroom scale; a small piece can be weighed on a food scale. Mark the weight and the date on the board after each weighing. When the wood stops losing weight it has reached its equilibrium moisture content with the outside air; it should then be brought indoors, where it should be further dried to an equilibrium moisture content consistent with the environment in which it will be used.

A more precise, though more expensive, method of monitoring moisture content is to use a moisture meter. Usually calibrated to cover a range from 6 to 30 per cent, such a meter determines moisture content by measuring the electrical resistance between two pin-type electrodes that are driven into the wood.

Lumber is customarily dried to a moisture content of 12 to 16 per cent; but for furniture-making and joinery, a moisture content of 6 to 8 per cent is recommended, depending on local climate and humidity. To minimize the problems caused by moisture variation, coat the finished piece with a moisture-impervious sealer to prevent dimensional changes.

# How Wood Responds to the Drying Process

**A predictable pattern of shrinkage.** Cuts of lumber, superimposed in their original positions on a log, show how wood tends to shrink unevenly as it dries, causing variations in shape. The greatest change occurs in a tangential cut, which closely parallels the direction of the annual rings. A radial cut, perpendicular to the rings, shrinks half as much. Uneven shrinkage across and along the grain of the rings causes circular cuts to dry to ovals, square cuts to diamonds.

**Changes in shape.** When wood dries too rapidly, the normal pattern of shrinkage is exaggerated and the board warps. Although considered defective to some degree, warped boards can often be salvaged by planing or, in more extreme cases, by steaming and redrying. The most common kinds of warping are cupping, springing, bowing and twisting. In cupping, the board curves into a hollow across the grain; in springing, the board lies flat but bends along the edges like a hockey stick; in bowing, the board arches from one end to the other; in twisting (also called winding), the board lies flat at one end but cups or springs at the other end.

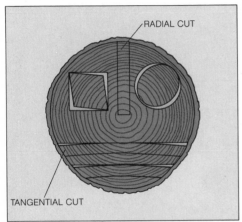

RADIAL CUT

TANGENTIAL CUT

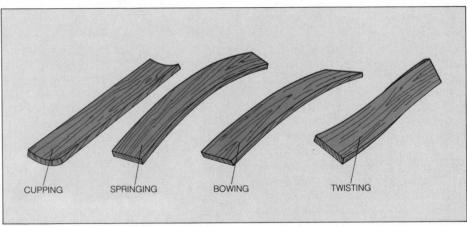

CUPPING          SPRINGING          BOWING          TWISTING

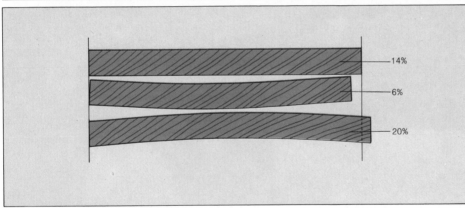

14%

6%

20%

**Changes in dimension.** As wood dries below the fiber-saturation point, it responds to variations in moisture content much as a sponge does, shrinking and swelling. In the top drawing, a board has been air-dried to 14 per cent moisture content, a standard amount for stock lumber. In the middle drawing, the same board has been dried to 6 per cent moisture content for cabinetry and woodworking, and has shrunk in width; it has also begun to cup slightly. At the bottom, exposed to a humid environment, the board has reabsorbed enough water to bring its moisture content to 20 per cent; it has swollen and has begun to cup in the opposite direction.

## A Probe for Measuring Moisture Content

**Using a moisture meter.** Plug the probe cord into the resistance meter, switch on the battery, and rest the pin electrodes against the board, parallel to the grain. Push down to insert the pins in the board to a depth equal to a quarter of the board's thickness. If testing a board thicker than 3 inches, insert the pins on both face surfaces and along the edges to a depth of 1 inch. Probe at several points along the board at roughly 12-inch intervals, avoiding the ends of the board and the areas around knots, which give up moisture quickly. Then average the readings, which may vary 2 to 3 per cent.

# Cutting Wood to Rough Length and Width

The first step in any woodworking project is to cut the wood roughly to the dimensions required for surfacing, shaping or joining. The initial cuts will also produce boards with straight edges and eliminate many defects that could cause problems later.

Whether you are working with milled boards from a lumberyard, old barn siding or chunks cut from logs, a table saw, the basic large machine in a woodworking shop, is the best tool for cutting boards to width (by ripping) and length (by crosscutting). A typical home model, with a blade 10 inches in diameter, can cut through boards up to 3¼ inches thick. Two saw accessories, the rip fence and the miter gauge, enable you to cut milled lumber to precise widths and angles, and easily made plywood jigs (opposite) will hold irregularly shaped pieces of wood in position for cutting straight edges.

You can get the best results with a table saw if you use the correct blade for the job at hand. A table saw commonly has a combination blade, which can be used for either ripping or crosscutting. However, a blade ground specifically for one job will give a smoother cut on that job. You can improve the performance of any blade by cleaning it periodically with a resin solvent such as turpentine, to prevent binding.

Vibrations from normal use can cause small alignment errors in the adjustable parts of a table saw. The tilt of the blade and the angle of the miter gauge should be reset before each project (right).

You should also periodically check the alignment of the saw table with the blade. To do this, unplug the saw, raise the blade fully and mark one tooth with a crayon. Then rotate the blade by hand so that the marked tooth is even with the table surface at the front of the blade slot. Measure from that tooth to each miter-gauge channel. Then rotate the blade until the marked tooth is at the back of the slot, and measure again. If the front and back measurements are not identical, adjust the tabletop according to the manufacturer's instructions—usually by loosening the bolts connecting the table to the base, tapping the tabletop with a rubber mallet until the alignment is perfect, then tightening the bolts.

Use a similar technique to align the rip fence before each ripping job. Position the fence so that the distance from the fence to both the front and the back edges of the saw blade is exactly the width of the planned cut. (Measure to the inner point of a saw tooth closest to the fence.) Lock the fence in place.

Careful selection and careful cutting will enable you to use wood economically. For example, if you are sawing an irregular piece that tapers from one end to the other, you will get the most from it by cutting it to rough lengths before ripping off the edges; you can then cut wider boards from the broader parts of the piece. Also plan your cuts to eliminate knots, cracks or other defects in the wood. When sawing around problem areas, use extreme caution. Knock out loose knots before sawing, to prevent their being thrown by the blade. Sawing through cracks can cause a wedge of wood to pop out with great force.

## Aligning the Saw for Precision Cuts

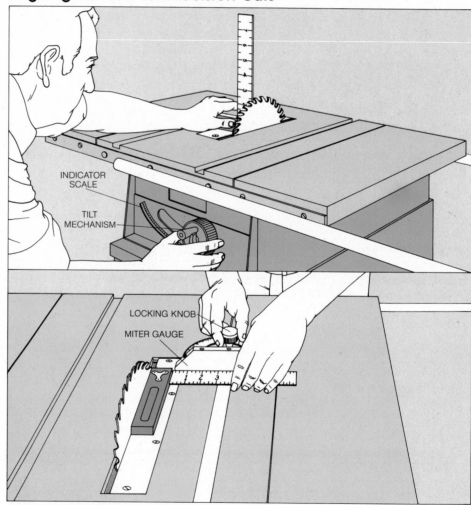

INDICATOR SCALE

TILT MECHANISM

LOCKING KNOB

MITER GAUGE

**Adjusting the blade and miter gauge.** To check the vertical alignment of the blade (top), unplug the saw, extend the blade fully and set a try square on the table, its tongue vertical against the blade. Use the saw's tilt mechanism to bring the blade flush against the square. If the blade does not move easily, check the track of the tilt mechanism for obstructions. When the blade is perpendicular to the table, adjust the pointer to 0° on the tilt mechanism's indicator scale.

For a 90° angle on the miter gauge (bottom), hold a try square's tongue against the miter gauge and its handle against the saw blade. Pivot the gauge to bring the square's handle flush against the blade, then tighten the locking knob.

# Jigs to Help Make Irregular Pieces Regular

**A crosscut jig.** A boxlike jig holds an irregular piece of wood in position for crosscutting on a table saw *(page 16)*. The base of the jig is made of ½-inch plywood, about 20 by 30 inches. It slides across the saw table on hardwood runners cut to fit into the miter-gauge channels. The runners are attached to the base of the jig with countersunk wood screws. Four-inch-high hardwood fences are glued and screwed to the top of the base, perpendicular to the runners. To cut a saw slot into the base and the fences, put the runners into the miter-gauge channels and slide the jig across the moving blade.

**A ripping jig.** A long, narrow jig is used to rip-cut a straight edge on one side of an irregularly shaped piece of wood; this straight edge can then be held against the rip fence as the opposite edge of the board is cut *(page 16)*. The 6-foot-long plywood base of the jig is guided by a single hardwood runner that fits into the miter-gauge channel to the left of the saw blade. The runner is positioned so that the right-hand edge of the jig's base is 1 inch from the blade; the runner is attached with countersunk wood screws. A 2-inch-high plywood cleat, used to hold the rough lumber in place on the jig, is screwed to the back end of the base, perpendicular to the runner. Two pieces of coarse sandpaper glued to the top of the base also help keep the rough board from shifting as it is sawed.

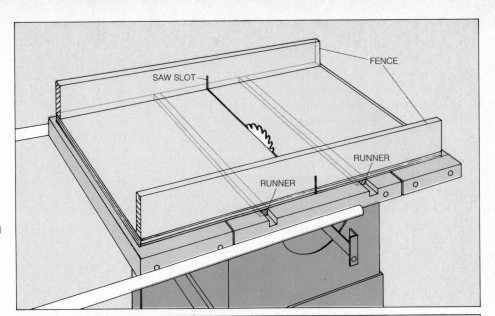

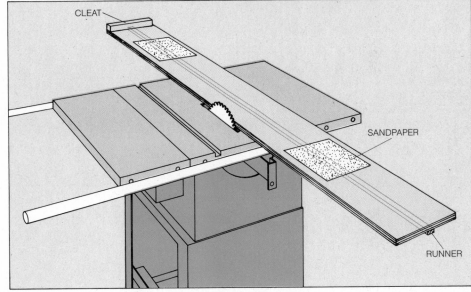

---

## Guidelines for the Safe Use of a Table Saw

Before you operate a table saw, familiarize yourself with the general rules for power tools *(page 9)*. Be sure to follow these specific safety guidelines for the saw:

☐ Keep the surface of the saw clean and free of wood scraps and tools. Keep the working area around the saw clear and well lighted.

☐ Use a push stick whenever you are ripping narrow stock. The stick is placed on the stock between the blade and the fence and is used to push the stock completely past the blade.

☐ Stand off to one side of the path of the saw blade.

☐ Hold the wood firmly against the fence or the miter gauge while cutting. Avoid awkward hand positions that will be hard to hold during the cut.

☐ Provide support at the sides or end of the table when cutting large stock.

☐ Do not remove the blade guard unless you are using a jig that cannot be moved through the guard; replace the guard immediately after making the cut.

☐ Before crosscutting, remove the rip fence from the saw table.

☐ Do not begin a cut until the blade has reached full speed; do not remove the stock until the blade has come to a complete stop.

☐ Never saw boards freehand; always use the rip fence, the miter gauge or a jig as you cut.

☐ Do not try to force a stalled blade while the motor is running; if the blade stalls, turn off the saw immediately.

☐ Never reach over the blade.

## Straight Edges for a Rough Board

**1** **Ripping the first rough edge.** Place the ripping jig *(page 15)* on the saw table and lay the board on the jig with one end butted against the cleat, the other end just in front of the blade. Then turn on the saw and carefully push the jig across the table, using one hand to press the board down against the jig's base.

**2** **Ripping the second edge.** Position the rip fence to guide the cut, then put the board on the saw table with the newly cut edge against the fence and one end just in front of the blade. Turn on the saw and slowly push the board into the blade with your right hand, initially pressing the board against the fence with your left. When your hands approach the blade guard, push the board with a piece of scrap wood or a push stick held between the saw blade and the fence.

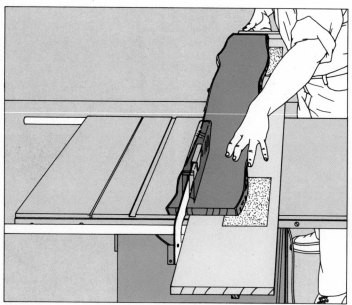

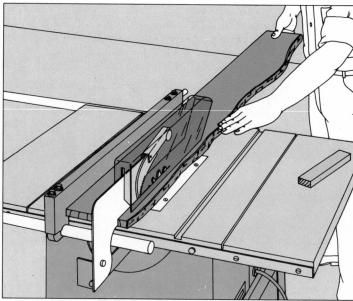

## Cutting Square Ends on a Rough Board

**Crosscutting with a jig.** Position the crosscut jig *(page 15)* on the saw table, then lay the rough board on the jig with one side against the fence near you and the marked cutting line over the saw slot. Switch on the saw and push the jig across the table with one hand, using the other one to hold the wood against the base and the fence. Keep both hands well away from the blade.

To crosscut several short pieces of identical length from one board, clamp a block of wood to the nearer fence of the jig; position the block so that the distance between the saw slot and the end near the slot is the same as the length of the boards to be cut *(inset)*. Hold the wood against the fence and the stopblock, turn on the saw and push the jig across the table. Turn off the saw, remove the cut piece, and return the jig to the front of the table. Reposition the board against the stopblock and repeat.

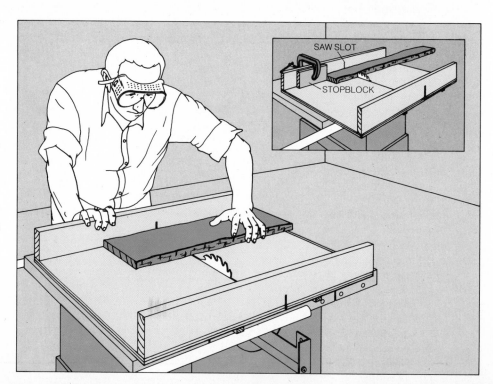

# Thin Boards from Thick Ones

Rough stock often is thicker than you want. You can get the largest number of usable boards from such wood by resawing it—cutting it into thinner boards. Resawing also allows you to make two pieces that have mirror-image grain patterns or to cut very thin slices of wood for use in veneers or inlays.

Although it is possible to resaw wood with a table saw or even a handsaw, the best tool for this job is the band saw. Most band saws designed for home use will cut wood up to 6 inches thick; because the blade is thin, a minimum of wood is lost as sawdust. Most home band saws have a high blade speed—about 3,000 feet per minute—which is excellent for resawing. A skip-tooth blade, so called because it has widely spaced teeth, is best for this fast cutting. Select the widest blade the saw will accommodate; a blade at least ½ inch wide will facilitate straight sawing.

After installing a new blade—and periodically while you are using the saw—check the blade's tension; a loose blade will not cut smoothly. To check the tension, run the saw briefly to seat the blade on the wheels, then unplug the motor and open the upper-wheel door. With a finger, push the blade to the right. If there is a deflection of more than ¼ inch, use the tension knob to adjust the upper wheel so that the blade is tightened.

Because the flexible blade tends to track along the wood's grain, you will need to guide the wood carefully as you cut. The L-shaped jig illustrated on page 18 provides a guide that allows precise manipulation of the wood for a straight cut. The vertical arm of the jig should be as high as the wood being cut; the leading edge of the vertical arm should be beveled to provide a pivot point.

Before you begin to cut, make sure that one edge and one face of the stock are square and straight *(page 16)*, so that they bear accurately against the saw table and the jig. The faces that are cut will be left rough by the saw blade, so they must be planed smooth. Because most resawed boards warp slightly as they dry, wait two or three days before you plane them to their final dimensions.

## Safety Rules for Band-Saw Use

The band saw is one of the safest shop tools when it is properly used. But in addition to the general safety rules that apply to all power tools *(page 9)*, users of band saws should be sure to observe these precautions:

☐ Mount the blade properly, so that the teeth are pointing down, in the direction the blade moves.

☐ Set the blade guides no more than ¼ inch above the wood you are cutting, to protect your fingers and provide maximum support for the blade.

☐ Avoid backing up in a cut. This could pull the blade off the wheels.

☐ Hold the stock firmly against the table and against any fence or jig you are using. If you have a helper supporting a cut piece, you still must control the cut by pushing and guiding the stock.

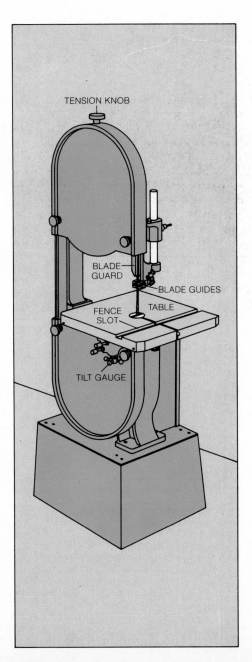

TENSION KNOB

BLADE GUARD

BLADE GUIDES

FENCE SLOT

TABLE

TILT GAUGE

**The versatile band saw.** Because it makes a wide range of cuts, from resawing thick stock to cutting delicate curves in thin strips, the band saw is a valuable woodworking asset. A typical home-shop band saw is 5 to 6 feet tall with a throat—the space between the blade and the arm—10 to 14 inches wide. The maximum amount of blade that can be exposed is usually just over 6 inches.

The blade is a flexible steel loop that passes around two large wheels, the lower wheel connected to an electric motor, the upper wheel turning freely to guide the blade and keep it taut. The table can be tilted 45° to the right, and most models have channels for such accessories as a miter gauge and a fence. A tension knob raises or lowers the upper wheel.

## Setting Up a Band Saw for Precision Cuts

**Adjusting the table and the blade.** To check that the blade is properly aligned with the table, hold the handle of a try square against the side of the blade so that its tongue is flush against the table. Adjust the table if necessary, then reset the table-tilt gauge at 0°.

Turn the adjusting screws on the upper and lower blade guides to bring the guides into position against the sides of the blade, then loosen these guides until you can slip a piece of paper between each guide and the blade. Inspect the blade from its side to be sure that the blade teeth, pointing downward, are visible in front of the guides and that the back of the blade does not touch the blade-support bearing *(inset)*.

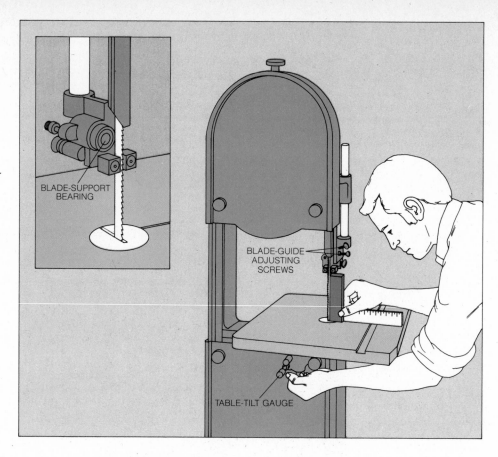

BLADE-SUPPORT BEARING

BLADE-GUIDE ADJUSTING SCREWS

TABLE-TILT GAUGE

## How to Resaw a Board

**1 Setting up for the cut.** Scribe a pencil line on the top edge of the stock to mark the thickness desired. Set the stock on edge on the table, with the end of the mark lined up with the teeth of the blade; align the jig *(inset)* to form a right angle with the stock, so that the jig's beveled nose is even with the teeth of the blade and with the edge of the stock. Clamp the jig securely in this position. Set the blade guides ⅛ inch higher than the top edge of the stock.

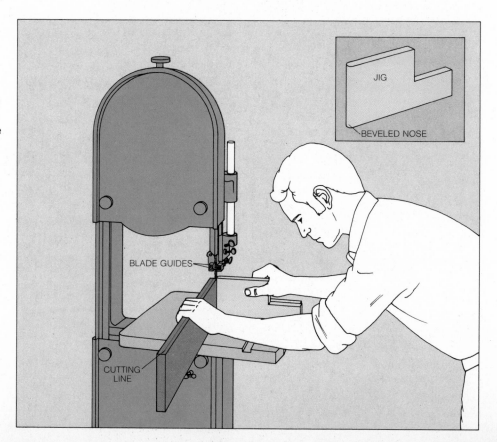

JIG

BEVELED NOSE

BLADE GUIDES

CUTTING LINE

**2 Starting the cut.** With the stock clear of the blade, switch on the saw. Then begin pushing the stock forward with your right hand so that the blade enters it on the cutting line. Use your left hand to press on the left side of the stock, opposite the beveled nose of the jig. If the blade twists away from the cutting line, use your right hand to pivot the stock against the nose of the jig, thus realigning the blade with the line.

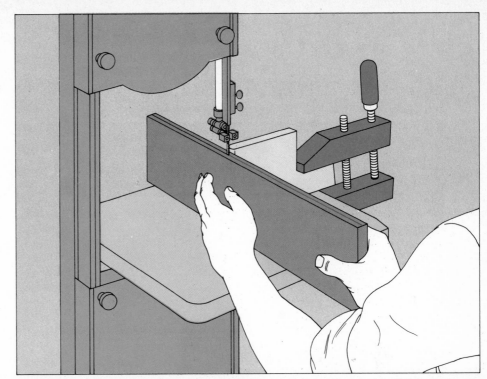

**3 Finishing the cut.** As you near the end of the cut, use a notched push stick to guide the stock through. Maintain pressure against the side of the stock with your left hand, but move the hand forward with the stock to avoid any danger of touching the blade at the end of the cut. Have a helper catch the far end of any piece too unwieldy for you to support as it comes off the table.

PUSH STICK

# Mirror-Smooth Surfaces Cut with Hand Planes

Once wood has been sawed roughly to size, more precise tools and techniques are required to achieve a smooth finish and exact dimensions. Any errors you make at this second stage can give the finished work a poor appearance or ill-fitting joints. You can attain precision surfacing using nothing more than hand planes; with good tools and practice, you can achieve mirror-smooth, perfectly flat surfaces on almost any piece of rough wood. The same tools also make it possible to salvage seemingly useless pieces by making straight, true boards out of twisted or warped wood.

Modern bench planes, each designed for a specific job, are the precision tools needed. A 14-inch-long jack plane is adequate for smoothing most lumber. If you have many rough boards to work on, however, you should consider starting with what is called a scrub plane, a tool that has a wood or steel body and a slightly convex blade designed to remove more wood with each stroke. The 20- to 24-inch body of a jointer plane suits it especially for surfacing boards longer than 2 feet, since it ensures a flatter surface by preventing the plane from following the original surface contours of the board. The small block plane, a one-handed tool only 6 inches long that has a shallow blade angle, is the best tool to use for smoothing the ends of boards.

Any board being planed must be firmly secured to your work surface. When you plane edges and ends, a vise and clamps are sufficient. For wider work surfaces, good workbenches often have holes to hold bench dogs—wood or metal pins that project slightly above the work surface and provide stops you can push the work against. Or you can improvise stops by nailing pieces of plywood, thinner than the board you are planing, to the work surface at each end of the board.

A perfectly flat work surface is essential, to let you check the flatness of the boards to be planed. If your bench is uneven, cover it with ½-inch or ¾-inch particleboard, using thin wood shims below it as needed to make it flat.

The techniques of hand planing can be perfected only with practice. To avoid the problems that develop if you plane against the grain of a surface or an edge, begin with a test. Set the plane blade for a shallow cut and take a few strokes in each direction. The direction that gives the smoother cut is the one to use when planing. When you plane a long surface, stand beside the workbench with your outer foot braced in front of you and your shoulders and hips parallel to the plane. To avoid rounding off the corners, be aware of the pressure you apply to the plane throughout each stroke. As you begin a stroke, press down on the front of the plane; press evenly as you plane down the length of the board; finish by pressing down on the rear.

As you work, check and adjust the plane blade frequently to make sure it is removing a minimum amount of wood. And as you adjust the blade, sight down the length of the plane's sole to check the angle of the blade as well as its depth; use the lateral adjusting lever on top of the tool to keep the blade edge exactly parallel with the mouth of the plane. Clean the sole with kerosene and lubricate it with candle wax; always set down or store the plane on its side to protect the blade.

Using a hand plane to smooth lumber to exact dimensions requires careful control. Begin by sawing or planing the board to within ⅛ inch of its final dimensions. Use a combination square and a pencil to mark reference lines; the scribed line of a needle-pointed instrument or a marking gauge is virtually invisible on rough wood. As you follow the penciled reference lines, keep in mind that the first face, edge and end can be planed until they are straight and perpendicular to each other, but the second face, edge and end must be planed exactly to the marked lines and no farther.

## Making the Faces Flat and Parallel

**1 Establishing a reference line.** Place a rough board on a flat work surface, and use a locking compass to mark a reference line as a planing guide on all edges of the board. If the rough board is cupped, place it concave side down; if it is twisted, keep it from rocking by placing thin wood shims under any corner that does not touch the work surface. Hold the compass with the pointed scribe touching the work surface and the pencil directly above the scribe, touching the board. Open the compass as wide as the gap where the least amount of wood must be removed, and lock it at this setting. Holding the pointed scribe against the work surface, slide the compass along the table to draw a pencil line around all four edges of the board. Keep the compass perpendicular to the work surface.

PENCIL

LOCK

SCRIBE

**2 Planing to the line.** Turn the rough board over, and secure it to the work surface with bench dogs or planing stops. Adjust a jack plane or a scrub plane for the first cuts, and begin planing off the high points—the parts of the board that have the greatest thickness above the reference line. Plane diagonally across the grain (*inset, left*). Then plane at a right angle to the first cuts, to eliminate any remaining ridges (*inset, center*). Sight down the board frequently, to locate any other high spots.

As the surface of the board nears the reference line, adjust the plane for shallower cuts. For final smoothing, hold the plane at a very slight angle to the grain and move it in a direction parallel with the grain (*inset, right*).

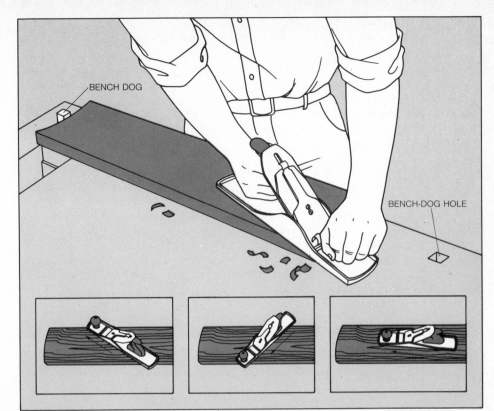

BENCH DOG

BENCH-DOG HOLE

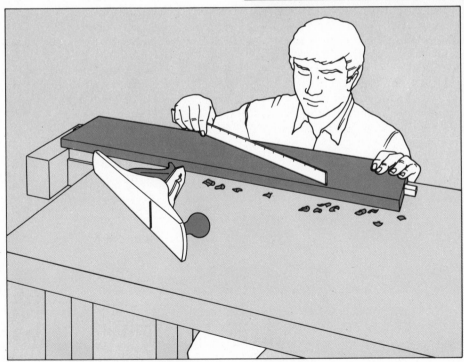

**3 Checking for flatness.** Set a straightedge rule on edge diagonally across the surface of the planed board. With your eyes nearly at the level of the board, slide the straightedge toward you. At low spots, light will show through between the straightedge and the board. Slide the rule at different angles across the surface to check for twisting. Plane down any remaining high spots.

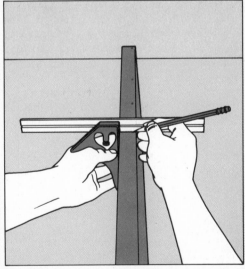

**4 Marking for planing to thickness.** When one face is smooth and flat, clamp the board on edge in a vise and use a combination square to mark the desired thickness on the edge of the board. Hold the head of the square flat against the planed side of the board, so that the ruler is crossing a long edge and is perpendicular to it. Mark that edge with pencil dots at the desired thickness, as measured by the ruler. Do the same with the other edge and the ends. Then connect the dots with a straight pencil line around all four edges of the board. Plane the second face to this line, starting at the high points as in Step 2. Check frequently for flatness, and be careful not to cut below the pencil lines.

# Squaring Edges and Ends

**1** **Planing a long edge.** Draw matching reference lines on opposite faces of the board and around the ends, as guides for planing the first long edge. Use a pencil and a straightedge to mark these lines about $1/16$ to $1/8$ inch in from the edge, then clamp the board in a vise with the marked edge up. Adjust the plane blade for the initial cuts and plane the edge, keeping the plane centered and square with the edge by placing your thumb on the plane's toe and using your knuckles as a guide along the smooth face of the board. Hold the plane so that its sole is parallel to the workbench and the plane is at a slight angle to the board's edge.

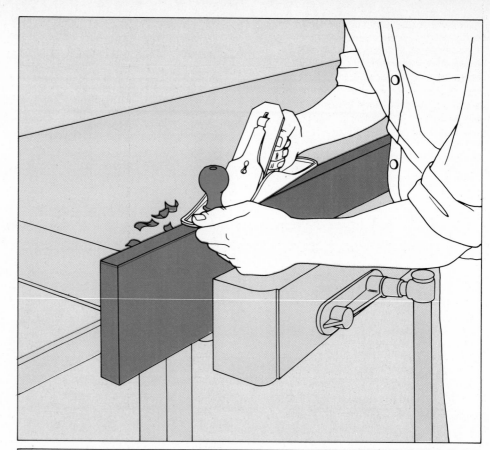

**2** **Checking for squareness.** When you have planed to within several strokes of the pencil lines, use a combination square to check the edge for squareness. Hold the board up to the light and, with the head of the square flat against the side, slide the square down the length of the edge, looking for any gaps. Mark any areas that are not square. Return the board to the vise and continue planing to the line, always using the shallowest possible blade setting and being especially careful to keep the plane level at the areas that are marked.

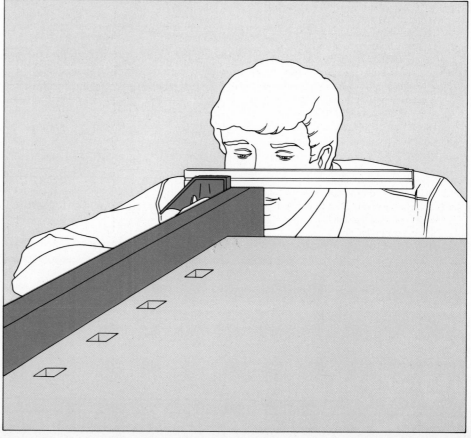

**3** **Marking the width.** With the board flat on the workbench, extend the ruler of a combination square to match the desired final width of the board. Place the head of the square against the planed long edge. Hold a pencil vertically at the end of the ruler, and slide the combination square and the pencil down the length of the board in one motion, marking a line that is parallel with the planed long edge. Repeat on the other side of the board. Using these reference lines, plane the second edge as you did the first.

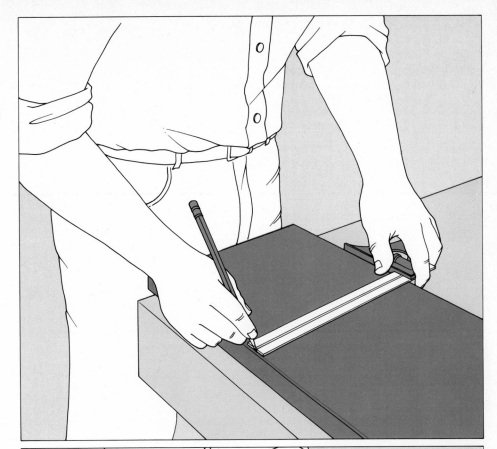

**4** **Planing the end grain.** Use a combination square to mark one end of the board with reference lines perpendicular to the long edges. Clamp the board flat on the workbench, allowing one end to overhang the bench edge by several inches. Set a block plane for a shallow cut; plane at a slight angle across the grain, using short, even strokes. To prevent chipping, plane from one edge to the middle; then turn the board over in the clamps, and plane from the other edge to the middle. Check for squareness as in Step 2, opposite.

Once the end is square, make very shallow cuts across the entire end to smooth and finish. Mark the opposite end of the board with reference lines at the final length of the board, and then plane it in the same manner.

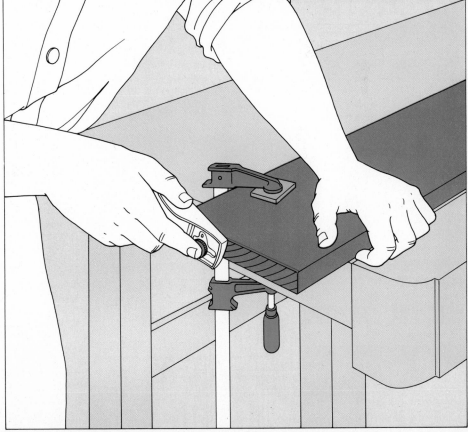

# Smoothing with a Power Planer

For smoothing and trimming wood, a motor-driven plane—called a jointer-planer or just a jointer—requires much less time and arm-wearying work than hand planes. The jointer is a precision machine designed to accurately shave small amounts of wood from faces, edges and ends of boards. The name derives from a common use of the tool for smoothing board edges so flat that when two are put together to form an edge joint, they match perfectly.

This precision results from the machine's design. Its cutter head, a revolving cylinder with two or three barely protruding blades, divides the jointer into two tables; the table closer to the operator is slightly lower than the far one. The highest reach of each blade edge matches the level of the far table. Thus, when a board is fed from the lower, near table into the cutter head, it is trimmed by the blades, then supported in its lessened thickness by the far table (*right, far inset*).

To ensure the most precise planing, the jointer blades should cut with the grain—although the board is fed toward the cutter head against the grain because the blades spin toward the operator. Also, the rate of board movement should be slow, and the depth of cut should be small—it is better to make several shallow cuts than a single deep one.

In addition to planing faces, edges and ends of boards—the three basic jobs described on the following pages—a jointer can be used to cut slanting bevels or chamfers along the edge of a board, step-like rabbets or projecting tenons at the end of a board. Bevels and chamfers can be cut when the tool's fence, mounted slightly above the tables, is tilted; rabbets and tenons are fashioned when the fence is moved partway across the cutter head, to a special rabbeting ledge that lets you guide pieces of wood partway on and partway off the cutter head.

Most home-shop jointers, though versatile and accurate, are not equipped to plane boards wider than 4 to 6 inches; never remove the blade guard in order to attempt planing wider boards, because such a procedure is very hazardous. There are jointers that will smooth 12-inch boards, but these are used mainly in professional shops. Heavy-duty planing can also be done on thickness planers, special machines that cut parallel surfaces. Both types cost several times as much as a home-shop jointer; most craftsmen take such kinds of planing to a millwork shop.

The blades on a home-shop jointer need sharpening when the shavings are limp, uneven and burnished-looking. Hone the blades with a few light strokes of a flat oilstone. Remove as little steel as possible—oversharpening can shorten the blade arc enough to put the blades out of alignment with the top of the back table. In time, you will need to have the blades ground professionally, then reset to a precise alignment with the tabletop. But you should periodically clean the blades—rub them with a cloth dampened in turpentine or lacquer thinner.

## Safety Precautions for Operating a Jointer

In addition to the general power-tool precautions on page 9, there are the following rules to be observed when you operate a jointer:
□ Unplug the machine when you are going to adjust its fence and tables or sharpen its blades.
□ Operate the jointer only when the blade guard is in place.
□ Do not plane pieces of wood less than 12 inches long; they may be pulled from your hands. If short pieces are needed, plane a long board, then cut it to the needed lengths.
□ Do not plane the face of a piece thinner than the height of the blade guard or ¾ inch, whichever is greater.
□ Use push blocks with any piece of wood less than 3 inches thick.

## A Tool Designed for Perfect Edge-Joinery

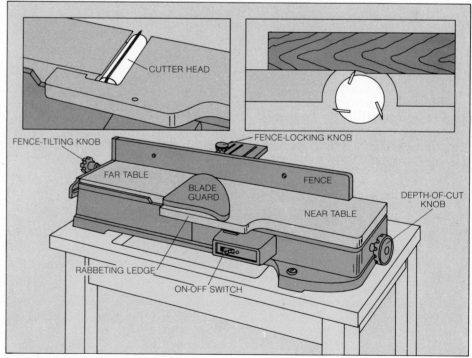

CUTTER HEAD

FENCE-TILTING KNOB

FENCE-LOCKING KNOB

FAR TABLE

BLADE GUARD

FENCE

DEPTH-OF-CUT KNOB

NEAR TABLE

RABBETING LEDGE

ON-OFF SWITCH

**A high-speed plane.** The jointer, mounted here on a stationary base, has a work surface 3 feet long. Its cutter head divides the table nearer the operator at the right from the far table at the left; the fence spans both. A spring-activated blade guard, removed in the left inset to expose the cutter head, is designed so that it will be nudged aside by boards passing along the fence and over the spinning blades but will still cover any unused portion of the cutters.

Three knobs adjust the jointer. The fence-locking knob can be loosened to allow the fence to be moved laterally, almost all the way to the near side of the table for use with the rabbeting ledge. The fence-tilting knob turns and locks the fence at angles from 45° to 135°, to serve as a guide in making chamfer and bevel cuts. The depth-of-cut knob is used for raising or lowering the table near the operator, to determine how much wood is planed from a board (*right inset*).

## Accouterments for Safety

**Push blocks and a high fence.** Two home-made push blocks are essential accessories for the safe use of a jointer. The smaller block is 3 inches square; the larger one is 6 by 12 inches and has a ½-inch-thick lip at one end. Both blocks are fitted with handles on top and pieces of rubber glued on the bottom; the rubber keeps the blocks from slipping as they are pushed against the wood.

Attached to the jointer here, but easily removed when it is not needed, is a 9-inch-high auxiliary fence made of ¾-inch plywood, sanded smooth and coated with paste wax to reduce friction. It is fastened to the machine's fence with screws driven from the far side through predrilled holes.

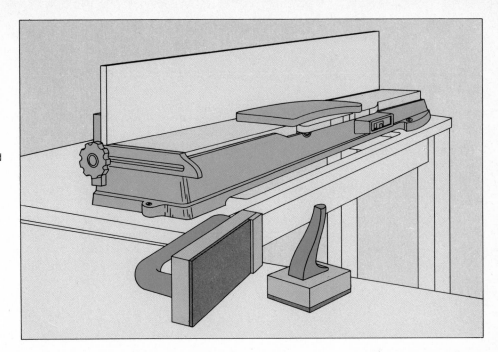

## Three Machine-made Cuts

**Planing the face of a board.** Stand to the left of the lower table, with your body angled about 45° toward the machine. Hold the lipped push block in your right hand at the back end of the board, the small push block in your left hand near the front of the board. Apply pressure down and toward the fence. Turn on the motor and feed the board forward at a slow, steady pace to deflect the blade guard and meet the cutter head. As the board progresses, maintain downward pressure on the portion over the higher table—if you inadvertently permit the board to tilt upward at the front end, you will get an unwanted taper. Maintain pressure down and toward the fence until the whole board has passed over the cutter head.

If the board is so long that the back end is beyond the reach of your right hand at the beginning of the cut, feed the board forward with your right hand while you use the small push block with your left. Pick up and use the lipped push block as soon as the back board end comes within reach, and finish the cut using both push blocks.

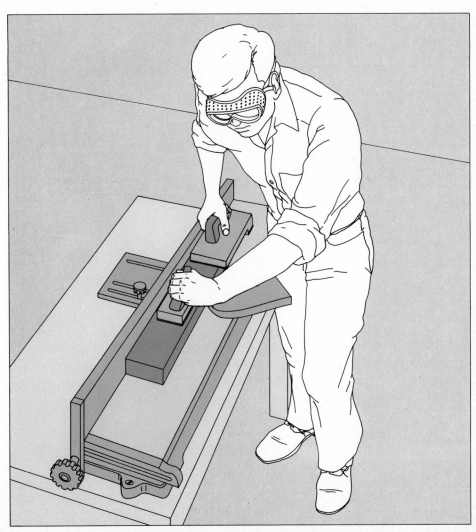

**Planing an edge.** Rest your left hand on the upper edge of the board and your right hand over the back end, if it is in reach. Push the board forward. Use your left hand to hold the board against the fence and down on the far table, your right hand to feed the board forward; keep both hands well away from the cutter head. Do not relax your pressure or change the slow, steady rate of feed until the cut is finished and your right hand is well beyond the cutter head.

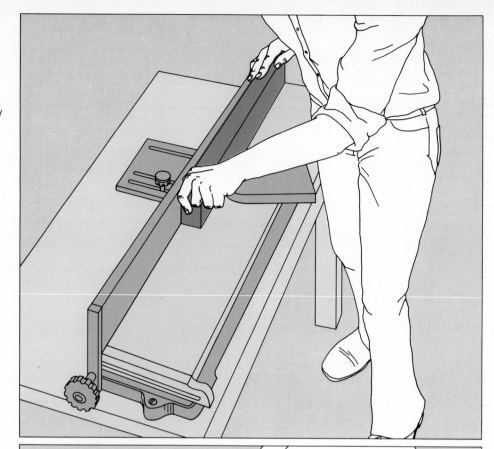

**Trimming an end.** With the 9-inch-high auxiliary fence in place, steady the upright board being end-trimmed with your left hand and push it forward with your right. After cutting about 1½ inches into the board (*inset*), stop the forward motion and pull the board slowly back onto the lower table. Reverse the board so that the cut portion is away from the cutter head, and push it all the way over the cutter head. This dual cut eliminates splintering at the end of the cut.

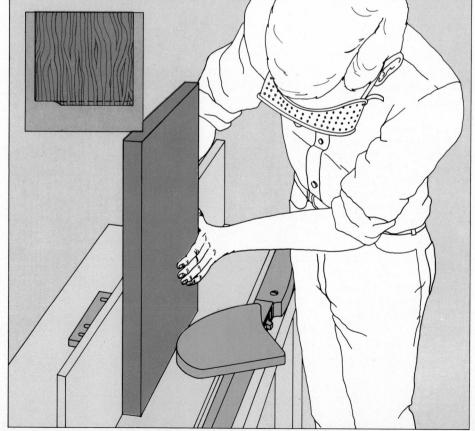

## Planing Defective Boards

**Removing a cup warp.** Place the board concave side down on the table nearer you, and feed it over the cutter head as for regular surface planing. Repeat this procedure on the same face as many times as it takes to make the face flat *(right, top)*. With the motor off, turn the board over, press it tight against the fence, hold a piece of scrap wood against the near edge, and mark the scrap where it touches the smoothed top of the board *(right, bottom)*. Using the pencil line as a guide, nail the scrap to the board edge so that it will keep the cupped board from rocking on its convex side. Feed both board and scrap across the cutter head repeatedly until the second face is flat and parallel with the first. (In both pictures, the blade guard has been omitted only for the sake of clarity.)

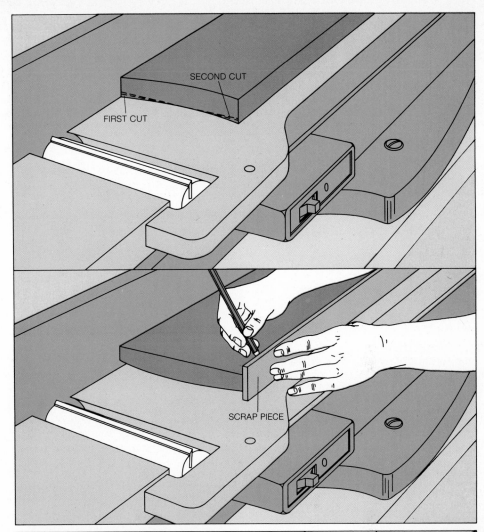

SECOND CUT

FIRST CUT

SCRAP PIECE

**Planing a twisted board.** Lay the twisted board on the table nearer you and then, checking with a small level, work triangular shims over and under the low corners of both faces *(inset)*. Trim the shims even with the edges of the board and glue them in place. After the glue has dried, run the board over the cutter head, but apply more pressure downward than against the fence. Plane one side until the shims on that side have been completely cut away, then repeat the same planing on the other side. (Note: In this picture, the blade guard has been omitted for clarity.)

Use this method only on boards considerably thicker than the deflection of the twist and, because the process is time-consuming, only on boards that are of value to you.

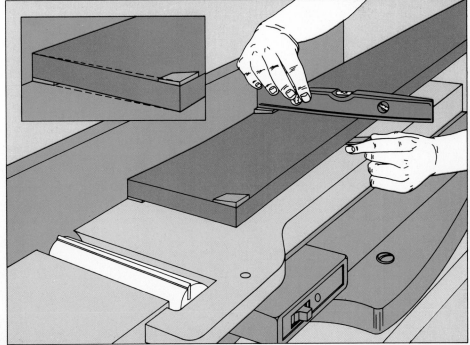

# Jointing by Hand to Produce Wide Panels

Before plywood came into common use in the 1930s, large wood panels were fabricated of several narrow boards fastened edge to edge. The simplest and most commonly used technique for such edge jointing, still used in fine cabinetwork, is to plane the edges of adjoining boards until they match exactly, then glue them together. If the boards are of equal thickness, the resulting panel will be smooth on both sides, with nearly invisible joints that are as strong as the wood itself.

By carefully selecting and matching the boards to be jointed, you can make a seemingly solid piece with a uniform grain pattern or a panel with alternating bands of wood color and grain. Or you can use boards cut from a single thick block of wood *(page 19, Step 2)*, to make a matched pattern in which adjacent boards seem to reflect each other.

In selecting the boards, choose well-seasoned wood to avoid shrinking, which could cause warping or opened joints. You can minimize the danger of warping in the finished panel by using narrow boards, only 4 to 6 inches wide, and arranging them so that the annual rings visible at the ends of adjoining boards curve in opposite directions.

The key to making perfect joints is careful edge planing. The technique of freehand planing with a jointer plane, 22 to 24 inches long, is similar to that used for planing the edge of any board, but the extra-long bed of the jointer plane helps ensure a straight edge without bumps or dips. This freehand planing requires practice to yield perfect results; but it allows you to change the planing direction, if necessary, to deal with reversal of grain direction, and to make small variations in the depth of cut to match adjoining pieces.

Until you master freehand planing, you may want to use a guide called a shooting board *(opposite)*. It guarantees a planed edge that is perpendicular to the surface of the board, and it provides an automatic depth stop so that you do not remove too much wood. It also allows you to use a plane with a bed shorter than that of the jointer plane.

Whichever planing method you use, be sure that the adjoining edges fit precisely. Any gap wide enough to allow light to pass through will greatly reduce the holding power of the glue.

White liquid glue, also known as polyvinyl acetate, is commonly used for edge jointing. It is strong, fills small gaps, and dries slowly enough to allow time for making fine adjustments. If greater moisture resistance is important, use yellow glue (aliphatic resin) instead; but note that this glue dries more quickly, so joints must be swiftly aligned and clamped.

Metal bar clamps, each with a pair of adjustable jaws mounted on an I-shaped bar, are the best choice for clamping edge-jointed panels; they flex less than similar pipe clamps or wooden bar clamps, thus ensuring flat clamping of a wide panel. Place thin wood scraps between the edges of the panel and the jaws of the clamps to avoid denting the wood. And to prevent stains that can be caused by a chemical reaction between the wood and the steel, put paper between the metal bars and the wood wherever they might touch.

## Matching and Planing the Panel Boards

**1** **Laying out the panel.** Position selected boards on a flat surface and align them to achieve the best possible grain pattern. Use a pencil and a straightedge to mark a three-line crow's-foot pattern from one side of the panel to the other, as a guide for maintaining the established pattern. Mark the ends of the boards at a point about 3 inches beyond the planned length of the finished panel, and cut off protruding boards at these marks to make them easier to handle.

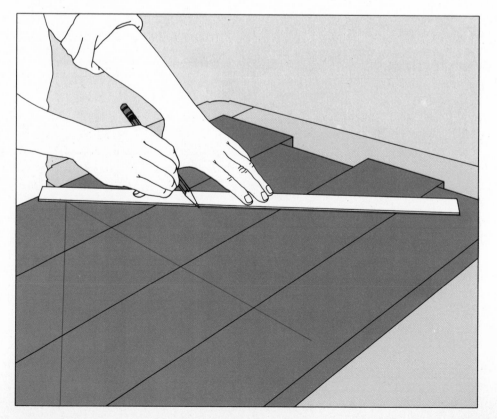

**2** **Freehand edge planing.** Clamp a board from one side of the panel in a vise so that its inside edge faces up. Using a jointer plane, test the edge (page 20) for the best planing direction, then begin at one end and plane the entire length. Gripping the nose of the plane with one hand will help ensure that the edge and the face of the board form a 90° angle. When the edge is straight and square, plane the matching edge of the next board in the same manner.

**3** **Testing matched edges.** With one board clamped in the vise, planed edge up, set the planed edge of the matching board on top of it with the crow's-foot marks aligned. Check the joint for nicks, gouges, and any gaps where light is visible. Use a pencil to mark the areas that need more work, then use a jointer plane to shave wood away until the edges match perfectly. Use the same techniques to plane and match the remaining pairs of edges in the panel.

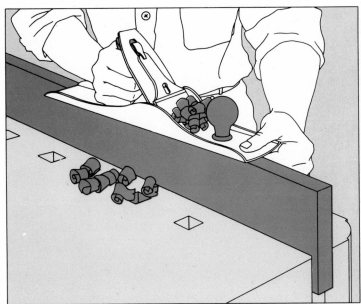

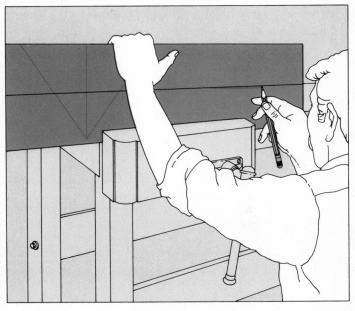

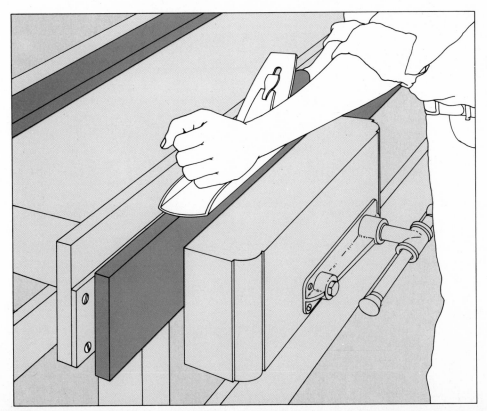

## A Simple Jig for Cutting a Straight Edge

**Planing with a shooting board.** Position the panel board to be edge-planed next to a shooting-board jig; clamp both in a vise, with the edge to be planed slightly higher than the depth stop of the shooting board. Plane from one end of the panel board to the other, keeping the side of the plane flush against the shooting board. Put wax on the side and bottom of the plane if there is a need to reduce friction.

To make a shooting board, cut a depth stop of ⅛-inch tempered hardboard, 3 inches wide and as long as the panel board, with one perfectly straight edge. Glue and screw this depth stop to the face of a straight 1-by-6 as long as the panel board, positioning the straight edge of the depth stop on top and keeping the bottom edges of the two pieces aligned.

# Gluing and Clamping for Smooth Beauty

**1** **Gluing the panel.** Apply a thin coat of glue to the planed edges of the boards to be joined. Lay the boards side by side on paper-covered metal bar clamps on a flat work surface. Fit each joint by sliding the glued edges back and forth, creating suction between the edges and working glue into the pores of the wood. Note the alignment of crow's-foot marks, but also attempt to match grain patterns on adjacent boards.

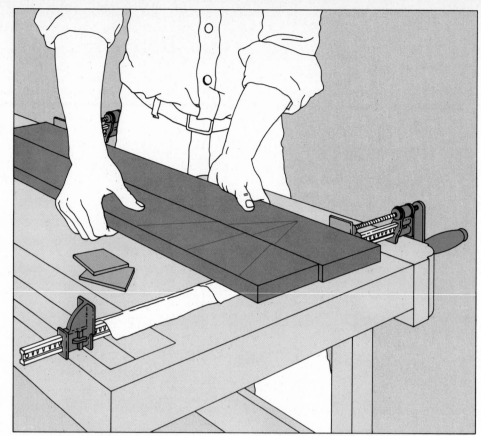

**2** **Adjusting the glued boards.** Tighten each of the bar clamps lightly against the assembly of glued boards. If any board is too high, tap it gently with a wooden mallet until the entire surface of the assembled panel is flush.

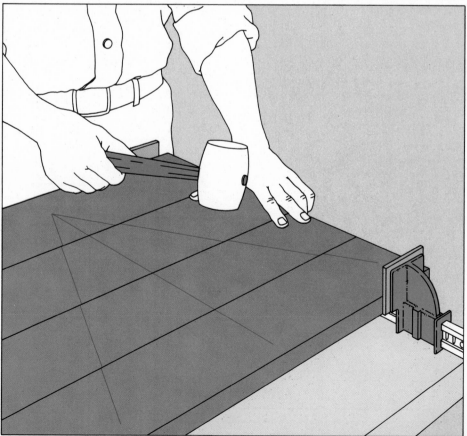

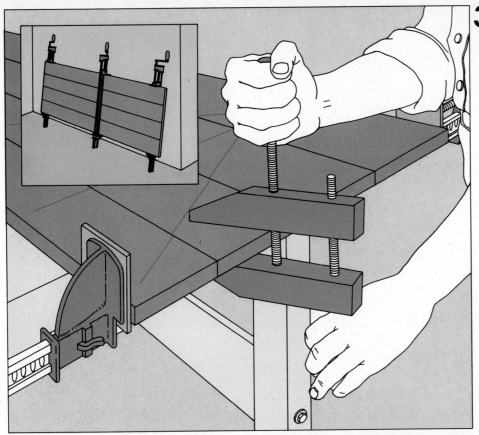

**3 Clamping the panel.** Using a hand-screw clamp with wood jaws, fasten each end of the glued panel to the middle of the bar clamp at that end. This will keep the panel from buckling when the bar clamps are tightened. On large panels, you can achieve the same result by using one or more bar clamps across the top of the panel, positioned between the bottom clamps. Tighten the bar clamps until a bead of glue is squeezed out of each joint. Clean this excess glue from the panel with a damp rag.

Store the glued and clamped panel flat, to keep it from twisting as the glue dries. If you lean the assembly against a wall (*inset*), make sure all clamp ends rest against both the wall and the floor. Allow the glue to set completely. Release the bar clamps first, then the hand screws, to avoid buckling the panel.

**4 Final planing.** Use a straightedge to check the flatness of the assembled panel (*page 21, Step 3*); plane down the high spots, if there are any. Then mark the thickness desired around the edges, and plane the panel to that line (*page 21, Step 4*).

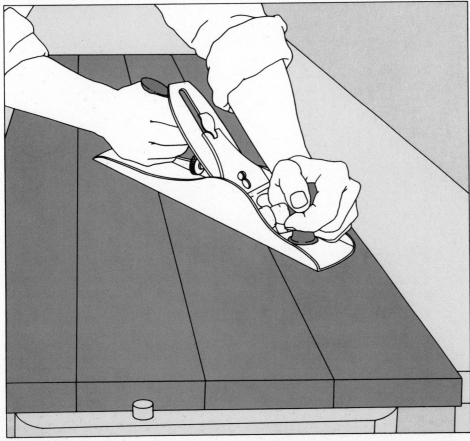

# Woodworking as an Art Form

In terms of contemporary life, the notion of handcrafted furniture stands out as a marvelous anachronism. Not since the beginning of the Industrial Revolution has there been any substantial market for scrupulously made, one-of-a-kind creations. Nor, in truth, has there been any great need to improve upon the basic design of the chair, the table or the storage receptacle; from a functional point of view, the mass-produced products serve us well enough. But to some artists, the making of furniture offers a mix of challenges and disciplines not to be found elsewhere. These advanced woodworkers ply their trade for the sheer pleasure of it.

That pleasure takes many forms. For George Nakashima, the American artist whose work is shown opposite, the process of furniture-making is essentially mystical. Nakashima regards wood as something "god-like" and he treats it with due reverence, creating "objects without style," furniture that uses extremely beautiful examples of nature's work in an all but untouched state.

To assure himself the most interesting stock from which to choose, Nakashima has made the collecting of wood an art form in itself. He personally selects his undressed timbers from sources around the world. On site at the sawmill, he studies each selection as a diamond cutter assesses a rough diamond, seeking the optimum cuts to get the most out of the material's unique natural beauty. Planks are then air-dried for two or three years, gently kiln-dried and finally sent to join some 20,000 other board feet of prize wood in Nakashima's sheds. There each plank stays for months, years, even decades, until the artist finds what he judges to be the perfect use for it.

Quite different, and in some ways opposed to Nakashima's approach to furniture-making, is the approach of the benders and laminators shown on page 36. These artists also have deep sensitivity for wood, but they see it as a material superbly responsive to being manipulated in various technical and sculptural ways. Recent advances in methods for bending and laminating wood, and in machine tools that can be made to slice and cut and bevel to tolerances of $1/64$ inch and less, have spurred them to invent furniture designs that are marvels at once of engineering and of organic form.

One offshoot of this furniture-as-sculpture school is the rarified group of artists who treat furniture as fantasy. Examples of their work (pages 38-40) range from the amusing to the bizarre—a desk in the shape of an elephant, a table whose top is permanently cluttered, chairs that are semiliteral translations of human and animal anatomy.

In contrast to the purist designs of a Nakashima, for example, the overlay of such personal caprice upon the nature of wood and the requirements of furniture verges on arrogance. But in their originality, these pieces make us uncomfortably aware of how anonymous, how impersonal, most conventional furniture has become; and for that insight and its challenge to do better, all designers (and all users of furniture) must be grateful.

**Planks of perfection.** A superbly executed trestle table is George Nakashima's chosen instrument for showing off a favorite pair of American black-walnut boards. Leaning against the walls of the artist's studio, awaiting similar skillful marriages, are planks of cherry, teak and several imported walnuts.

## When Wood Patterns Dictate Furniture Design

Wood with knotholes, burls, cracks, crotch-graining and extravagant color contrasts is often rejected by traditional furniture makers as too eccentric for their purposes. But to the artist-craftsman these aberrations are the stuff of creative imagination.

The key to the woodworker's success is his willingness to take his basic design direction from the raw materials—to go with the flow of grain and texture and color. In the examples shown here, the designers have left the wood in a nearly natural state, making only such minimal concessions to utility as smoothing the tabletops or scooping out seating.

**Soul of walnut.** A pair of 36-inch-wide, 2-inch-thick slabs of centuries-old English walnut provide a wildly patterned top for a table by George Nakashima. Reverse-matched to emphasize the wood's contrasting colors and grains, the slabs are joined along the interrupted center seam with rosewood butterflies.

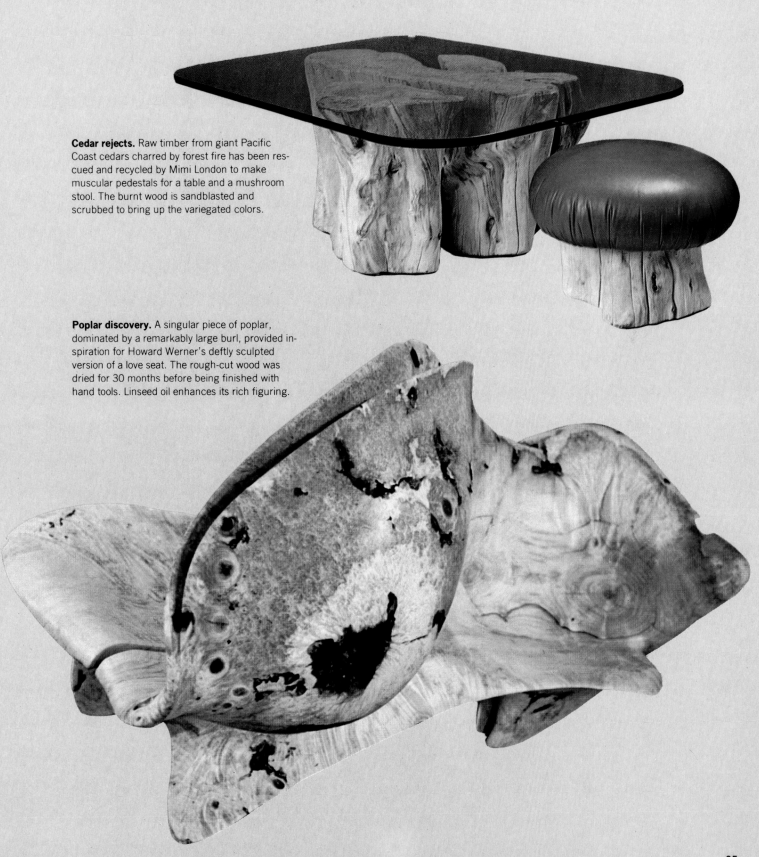

**Cedar rejects.** Raw timber from giant Pacific Coast cedars charred by forest fire has been rescued and recycled by Mimi London to make muscular pedestals for a table and a mushroom stool. The burnt wood is sandblasted and scrubbed to bring up the variegated colors.

**Poplar discovery.** A singular piece of poplar, dominated by a remarkably large burl, provided inspiration for Howard Werner's deftly sculpted version of a love seat. The rough-cut wood was dried for 30 months before being finished with hand tools. Linseed oil enhances its rich figuring.

## Opulent Abstractions of Nature's Curves

Supple, flowing lines and highly refined details characterize the one-of-a-kind furniture shown here. All reflect to some degree the fascination with curvilinear forms that marked the work of Art Nouveau modernists circa 1900. The dining furniture opposite, together with its co-ordinated wall paneling, belongs to the original movement. Most of its opulent ornamentation depends on simulations of bentwood—but the wood is sculpted rather than being structurally bowed.

By contrast, the designers of the contemporary pieces on this page have achieved fluid lines by actually bending, twisting and laminating thin layers of matching or contrasting wood. In the process, they have exploited techniques and materials unimagined a few decades ago. The result is furniture that gives full rein to the artist's imagination without sacrificing strength or stability.

**Compound curves in space.** Easily flexed ⅛-inch-thick strips of cherry were laminated and bent to create this asymmetric chair. Designer Seth Stem free-bent the flying curves, then pulled them taut and shaped them into arching legs. While the glue dried, the legs were secured by spiralling rubber ribbons cut from inner tubes.

**Laminated lounger.** Using short lengths of highly figured African mozambique, Michael Coffey built up and shaped as many as eight layers of wood to create his serpentine rocker. For stability he staggered the laminate joints and reinforced them with lighter-colored splines.

**Room in motion.** In keeping with the Art Nouveau penchant for perfect harmony, French cabinetmaker Eugène Vallin matched the furniture to this turn-of-the-century interior. He chose a single wood, citron, and duplicated the curvilinear shapes used in the moldings and mantelpiece.

## Taking Liberties with the Conventional

Throughout the history of furniture design, the notion of using unlikely ornament has always exercised a certain counterculture appeal. Fantasy furniture offers the artist an opportunity to happily reinvent utilitarian pieces and to create objects that are highly personal, highly visible and often fun to live with.

Three contemporary examples of such original works are shown here; a fourth, from an earlier day, appears on page 40. Just as the legs of ancient thrones mimicked the legs of lions, so two of these pieces play with animal and human forms. The table is a variant on a fashion for illusion popular in the 18th Century.

**Trompe l'oeil table.** Wendell Castle's jaunty rendition of a French 18th Century gaming table has a hat and scarf, seemingly tossed by a visitor, as permanent sculpted fixtures. The traditional table is made of African doussié; its witty additions are carved from laminated sections.

**Elephant desk.** Nearly 10 feet long from trunk to tail, this exuberant expression of the cabinetmaker's imagination was assembled and carved by Chris Schambacher. The beast is stacked strips of shedua, a dark African wood; the storage area and the tusks are worked in contrasting bird's-eye maple.

**Hand craft.** Giant-sized cupped hands are carved from laminated mahogany and gilded, as Pedro Friedeberg's artful contribution to chair design.

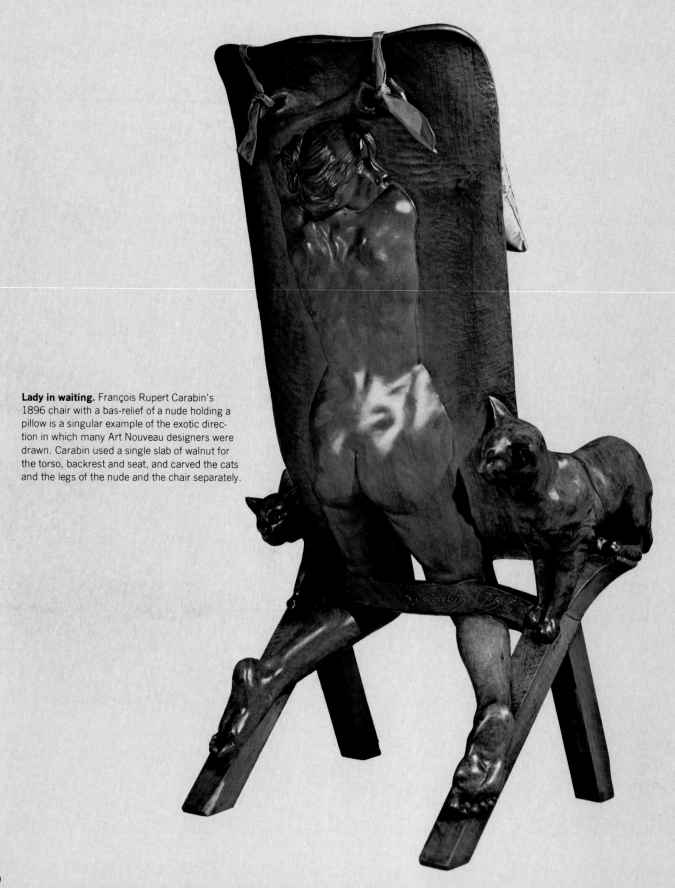

**Lady in waiting.** François Rupert Carabin's 1896 chair with a bas-relief of a nude holding a pillow is a singular example of the exotic direction in which many Art Nouveau designers were drawn. Carabin used a single slab of walnut for the torso, backrest and seat, and carved the cats and the legs of the nude and the chair separately.

# A Reverence for Tools and Joinery

In Japan, one of the most industrialized nations in the world, a sense of reverence still surrounds traditional woodworking tools—saws such as the ryoba, dozuki and azebiki—and the elaborate joints these delicate but precise instruments can fashion. Unlike its Western counterpart, Japanese joinery evolved not from furniture-making but from the construction of Shinto shrines and Buddhist temples. Consequently, the Japanese carpenter was once as much an architect as a woodworker.

For these craftsmen, respect for the tools comes above all else and is the key to fine woodworking. It was once considered a grave offense for an apprentice to step over a saw at a work site; he would be soundly slapped for his disrespect. As a part of his show of reverence for a tool, the woodworker must learn to use it with exquisite skill. This is not always easy. Japanese saws, for example, cut on the pull stroke, rather than the push stroke—the teeth face back, toward the woodworker, and this allows the blades to be thinner and lighter. The cut is more accurate since there is much less of a kerf, but using the saw requires more skill.

A good Japanese saw is both flexible and hard—some will bend into a half circle and still return to their original shape. The saws most used in woodworking shops are the ryoba, for rough cutting, and the dozuki, for more accurate work. The ryoba has two edges: one for crosscutting, with 15 to 20 teeth per inch, the other for rip cutting, with 6 to 8 teeth per inch. The dozuki resembles the backsaw or the dovetail saw and has 25 to 30 teeth per inch.

Saws range in length from 8¼ inches to 16½ inches for the ryoba, and from 8¼ inches to 12⅜ inches for the dozuki. The larger sizes are used for carpentry rather than cabinetmaking. The more specialized azebiki is shaped to cut openings in the center of panels; it has 10 teeth per inch on one edge and 15 teeth per inch on the other.

Other tools include a version of the keyhole saw, planes that—like the saws—are pulled rather than pushed, and chisels. The blades of these planes and chisels are made of a laminated composition of high-carbon and low-carbon steel, not solid steel. This composition allows them to absorb more shock and makes the blades easier to sharpen. One of the commonest Western tools, the vise, is often absent: Japanese woodworkers usually sit at low workbenches, only 1 or 2 feet above the ground, and for accuracy use hands, elbows, even legs and feet to hold the wood in place. This is possible because Japanese tools require so little force.

But it is the joints these tools fashion that make Japanese woodworking so extraordinary. Of the 400 joints still in use, many evolved from secret joints designed by competing guilds of carpenters, which no one outside the guild could reproduce. In Japan joints are called either splicing joints, in which pieces are joined end to end, or connecting joints, in which pieces are joined at an angle. Two of the joints below are splicing joints; the third, the jigoku-kusabi, is a connecting joint.

The mechigai-koshikake-kama-tsugi, roughly translated as "lapped gooseneck mortise-and-tenon joint with stub tenons," was once used to splice beams together. The kaneori-mechigai-tsugi, or "half-blind L-shaped stub tenon," is a complex blind mortise-and-tenon joint that skilled craftsmen use to join sections of wood without using nails. And the jigoku-kusabi—which literally means "hell's wedge"—is aptly named: The wedges in the tenon, when forced against the bottom of the mortise, are pushed back into the tenon, making the two pieces impossible to take apart. It is often used to join legs to tabletops and may be considered a Japanese alternative to the dovetail.

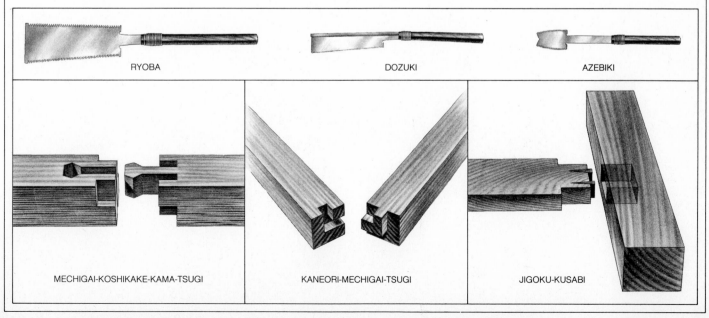

RYOBA

DOZUKI

AZEBIKI

MECHIGAI-KOSHIKAKE-KAMA-TSUGI

KANEORI-MECHIGAI-TSUGI

JIGOKU-KUSABI

# 2

# A Choice of Connections

**A tried-and-true connection.** The stalwart mortise-and-tenon joint possesses two characteristics that make a joint strong: ample gluing surface and resistance to stress. Both the slotted mortise and the protruding tenon were once cut by hand, but the mortise of a modern joint is typically made with a drill press *(background)*, which reams out a series of overlapping holes; the rounded edges are then squared with a chisel.

The quality of a piece of furniture is judged by the beauty of its form and the strength of its parts—and joinery plays a major role in both. More than just a means of locking together two pieces of wood, a joint can merge component parts with grace or set them off in fine contrast to each other. It can guide the eye along the lines of a piece, as in a miter joint, which allows the grain to flow unbroken around the corner; or it can delineate the change of direction, as in a lap joint. It can combine in itself both function and esthetics, arresting the eye with such intricate details as the winglike wedges of the dovetail joint or the contrasting wood of exposed dowel joints. Conversely, a joint may exert no visual effect, being completely hidden—as the invisible mortise-and-tenon joint is.

Faced with a multitude of choices, most woodworkers elect to use the simplest, strongest joint appropriate to the job. All joints, regardless of how they are cut, derive some of their strength from the amount of gluing surface they provide. The strongest joints are those that connect two pieces of wood in a way that bonds the greatest possible surface of lengthwise grain on each piece. The long grain, running with the wood fibers, holds glue in suspension, ensuring a strong bond; the end grain, cutting across the fibers, is so porous that it simply absorbs the glue and offers practically no gripping surface. Some joints do not expose as much long grain as others. A miter joint, for example, cuts diagonally across the end grain and usually has to be reinforced with a spline to increase its holding power.

In fact, because most joints can be given the requisite strength, the choice of joint usually boils down to how much time and skill it takes to cut and fit it. Hand-cut dovetails take considerably longer to make than machine-cut dovetails, and machine-cut mortise-and-tenon joints are simpler and speedier still—which is why most craftsmen choose the latter. Even simple joints demand precision cutting. No woodworker should cheat on the time spent in marking and measuring the cut. Sharp hand tools and well-honed power-tool blades and bits are also essential to the clean cuts of good joinery.

Finally, for a joint to be both smooth and serviceable, its parts must fit together as precisely as possible. In a good joint, no light shows between the pieces—proof that the gluing surfaces mate. The snugness of fit should be such that some hand pressure is needed to bring the pieces together, or a light tap with a mallet or a hammer and block. But the fit should not be so tight that wood fibers are forced out of place. In earlier days the strength of a joint depended primarily upon the tight fit of its interlocking parts. Today wood screws and sophisticated glues can supplement fit, not only strengthening the joint but increasing its life expectancy.

# The Tongue-and-Groove Joint and Its Variations

Cutting a groove in one board and fitting a projecting tongue from another into it is one of the oldest and still one of the best ways to make a strong wood joint. Two types of cut are used to make such a joint. One is the rectangular channel, called a dado, cut in either the edge or the face of a board. The other is a step-like cut, called a rabbet, made in the edge of a board. In a variation of the basic rabbet, two shallow rabbet cuts may be made, one along each side of a board edge, leaving a projecting center remnant, the tongue. Dadoes and rabbets can be combined in several ways to join boards, either at right angles or flush with each other *(below)*.

The tools most commonly used for making these cuts are the router and the table saw. Each has advantages in certain circumstances. For example, if you are cutting dadoes and rabbets in wide boards, plywood sheets, oddly shaped pieces or warped wood, the router is a better choice, since the wood remains stationary while the tool follows its contours. In these circumstances a table saw may fail to cut consistently deep, especially if the wood is warped. Moreover, it takes time to assemble the collection of saw blades and wood chippers, called a dado head, that is needed to cut wide dadoes and rabbets with a saw. Nevertheless, once a dado head is installed and adjusted, the table saw will be faster than a router for making identical cuts in a number of boards.

No matter which tool you choose, precise measurements are imperative. A keen eye and a perfectly straight rule are needed to make certain the cutting blades are exactly positioned. But even after careful measuring, every new blade setting should be tested on scrap wood. This extra effort pays dividends, especially if you are making intricate cuts like those in a lock joint *(page 49)*. To prevent plywood from splintering when cut with a table saw, you can either score the wood beforehand with a blade set very low or cover the location of the cut with a strip of masking tape.

If your project calls for a large amount of edge-to-edge joinery, there is an alternative to the tongue-and-groove joint: the glue joint. To make it with a table saw, you will need to install a special cutter called a molding head. It shapes, in a single pass, pairs of tongues and grooves in the edge of a board. Furthermore, without changing the adjustment you can shape the edge of the board that will be joined to the first one.

## Safety Rules for Routers

The high speed of the router's rotating bit demands that this portable tool be treated with the same respect as larger, stationary power tools. In addition to the general safety rules for all power tools *(page 9)*, observe these specific precautions for the router:
□ Unplug the tool before installing or removing a bit, and tighten the chuck securely after installation.
□ Anchor your work securely with clamps or nails, leaving both hands free to guide the tool.
□ Let the bit reach full speed before beginning a cut, and lift the bit from the work before switching the router off. But keep in mind that the cutter will continue to spin for several seconds after the router is switched off.
□ Whenever possible, move the router away from you and direct it so that the leading edge of the bit, which spins clockwise, is biting into new wood; position any guides or jigs so that they will counteract the resulting counterclockwise torque.

## Five Rabbet and Dado Cuts

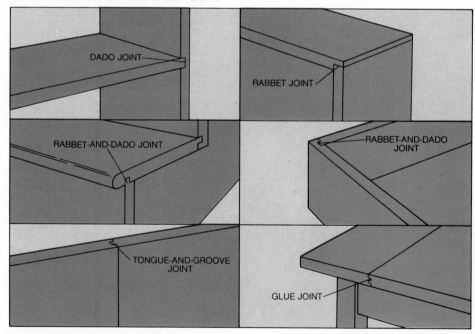

**A catalogue of joints.** The basic dado joint, shown in the drawing as it is used to hold shelves, is formed when the square end of one board is fitted into a channel-like dado in a second board. A simple rabbet joint, here used at the top corner of a box, is made by fitting the unshaped end of one board into the rabbeted end of the other. A rabbet and a dado may also be combined, with the rabbeted end of one board fitting snugly into the dado of another; this assembly appears as it is used in a stair tread and in the back of a drawer.

The tongue-and-groove joint, common in flooring and paneling, joins edges; a dado in the edge of one board holds the tongue left by cutting two shallow rabbets in the other. A fifth joint, the glue joint, is made with a special table-saw cutter; pairs of dadoes and rabbets with slanted sides provide interlocking gluing surfaces.

# Routing Out Grooves and Recessed Edges

**Routing a dado.** A T-shaped jig makes a useful guide when you rout a dado across the face of a board. First mark the position and depth of the dado, then hook the jig's crosspiece on the far edge of the board. To position the jig, raise the cutting bit above the router base, move the jig against the left side of the router, then move jig and router together until the bit lines up with the dado position. Clamp the jig and the wood in place; tack down the long end of the jig if clamping it is difficult. Lower the bit to the desired depth at the edge of the wood, turn on the router and move it into the wood. Lift it out when a notch has been cut into the jig's crosspiece.

Make the jig of smooth-edged wood about 3 inches wide and as thick as the board being dadoed. Use a square to position the jig pieces at right angles, then fasten them with screws.

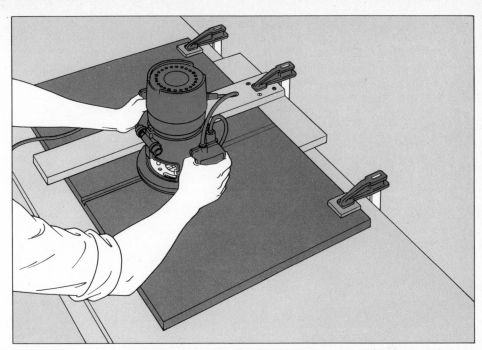

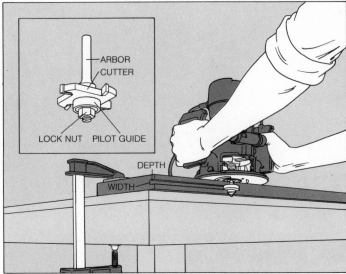

**A bit for routing edge grooves.** A special dado cutter, called a panel-grooving bit or a spline bit, is fitted with a noncutting pilot guide at its tip. This cylinder rolls along a board edge to ensure that the groove will be of uniform depth. To use this bit, mark the position of the groove, clamp the wood to a worktable edge, and lower the cutter until it lines up with the marks. Guide the bit into the wood from left to right. If you are cutting wood that may chip or splinter, such as plywood, begin the cut about 1 inch from the left end, and finish the remnant by cutting from right to left.

The groove's width will be determined by the size of the cutter; its depth depends on the diameter of the pilot (*inset*). Choose a small pilot for a deep cut, a large one for a shallow cut. Replace any pilot that feels rough or gritty.

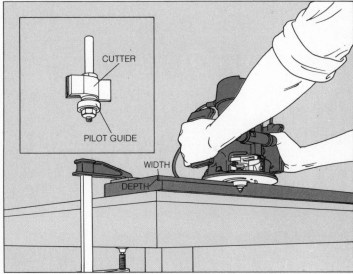

**Routing rabbets and tongues.** A rabbet cutter equipped with a pilot guide (*inset*) is used in the same way as the panel-grooving bit (*above, left*). Select a cutter-pilot combination that will produce a rabbet of the desired depth and width. Cut from left to right, but in this operation lower the bit gradually so that each pass removes no more than ⅜ inch of wood.

For a tongue of wood on the edge of a board, mark and cut two rabbets, one in each opposing face, so that the projection remaining is centered and has the desired thickness. Use a cutter-pilot combination that cuts a rabbet $1/16$ inch narrower than the depth of the groove.

# Adjusting a Table Saw for Cutting Dadoes

**1** **Installing a dado head.** Remove the standard table-saw blade from its arbor, and install the blades and chippers of a dado head. If the first dado blade has cocked teeth, angle them toward the arbor base. Add chippers and paper washers, aligning the chippers with the gullets of this blade (*below, left*). Add the second blade to make the combination of blades, chippers and washers as wide as the desired dado.

Align the gullets of the outside blade with the chippers, matching the position of the inside

blade. If the blades have teeth of two sizes, align the smaller teeth of one blade with the larger teeth of the other. If the second blade has cocked teeth, they should angle away from the first blade. Lock the dado head in place with the arbor washer and nut.

Check the width of the dado head with the metal extension of a folding rule (*below, right*), measuring from the outside tips of the teeth. Make adjustments if necessary, then install a dado insert in the table-saw opening.

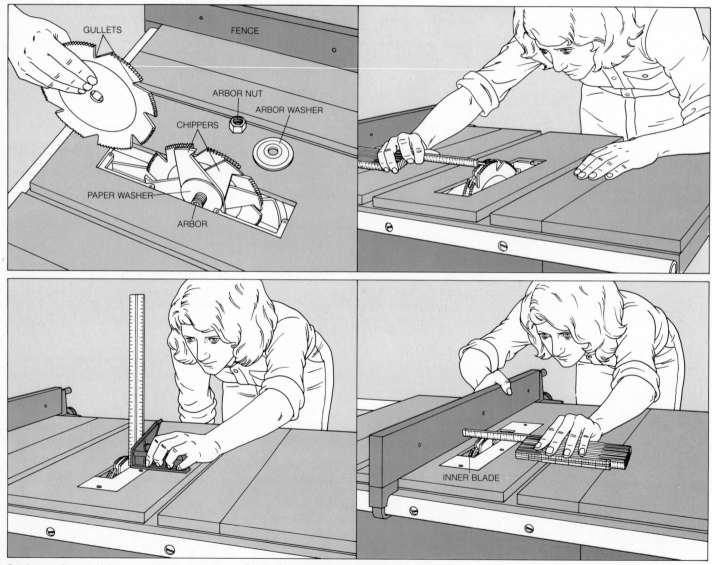

GULLETS

FENCE

ARBOR NUT

ARBOR WASHER

CHIPPERS

PAPER WASHER

ARBOR

INNER BLADE

**2** **Setting up the cut.** Using a combination square to check the height of the dado head (*above, left*), set the blades a fraction of an inch lower than the desired depth of the dado. Adjust the setting by making test cuts as needed (*Step 3*). Be sure to lock the blade-height crank after each adjustment you make.

Set the fence so that the distance between the fence and the inner dado blade equals the distance desired between the edge of the wood and the edge of the dado (*above, right*). If the tips of the teeth on the blade are cocked, measure from the fence to the side of a tooth that angles toward it. Lock the fence in place.

**3 Cutting the dado.** Make a test cut on scrap lumber, to verify that the dado has the correct width, depth and clearance from the board edge. To do this, let the saw reach full speed, then run the wood smoothly over the dado head: Feeding the wood too rapidly results in rough cuts and may cause a kickback; feeding it too slowly burns the wood. Stand to the left of the blade for safety in case of a kickback, pressing the wood against the fence with your left hand, down on the table with your right. Use a push stick if the board is narrow.

When the test dado is cut, check its dimensions and position with a ruler or with the piece of wood that will fit into it. Make further adjustments if necessary, until the saw is perfectly set. Then make the final cut in the work.

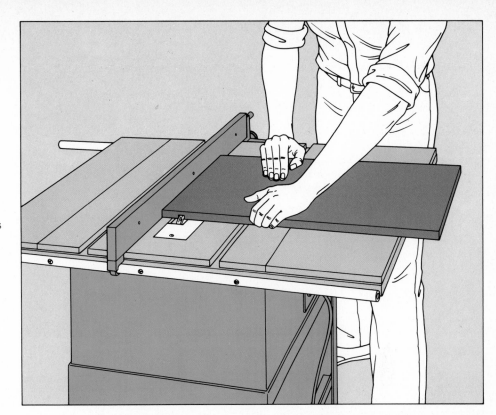

# A Rabbet Made on a Table Saw

**Using an auxiliary fence with a dado blade.** To make a smooth rabbet cut, assemble a dado head slightly wider than the desired width of the rabbet, set the blade height for the appropriate depth of cut, and pass the wood over the blade as for a dado cut. Before making the cut, fasten an auxiliary wooden fence to the metal fence, turn on the saw, and slowly raise the dado head. Notch the auxiliary fence to provide clearance for the small part of the dado head that extends beyond the work.

Make the auxiliary fence from smooth ¾-inch wood that is square at all edges. Hardwood plywood, particularly birch plywood, is a good choice because it is very smooth. Trim the wood to the dimensions of the metal fence, and fasten it with screws driven from the far side through the predrilled holes.

To make a tongue, follow the same procedures, but cut shallow rabbets in opposite faces of the board so that the tongue of wood remaining in the middle is of the desired width (*page 45*).

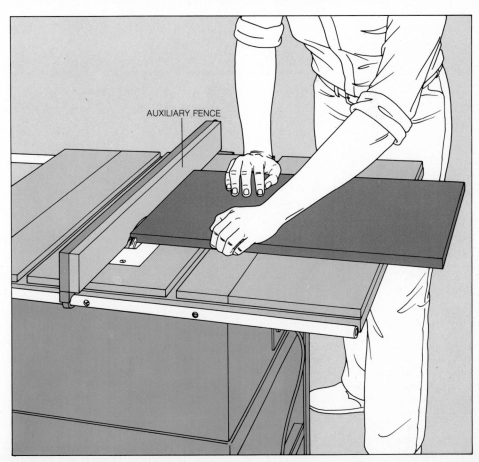

AUXILIARY FENCE

# Setting Up a Table Saw for a Glue Joint

**1** **Installing a molding head.** Slide the special glue-joint cutters completely into the molding-head slots, and lock each one securely in place by tightening its setscrew with a hex wrench. Remove the standard saw-table insert and blade; replace them with the molding head, any washer or bushing that goes with it, and a molding-head insert. Add an auxiliary wooden fence, and notch it with the cutters (*page 47*).

With the saw unplugged, sight along the top of the table while you turn the molding head with your left hand and adjust the height of the blade with your right. The blades are at the correct height when the bottoms of their recesses are on a level with the tabletop. Before you begin to cut, make marks on the boards to indicate which of the edges are to be joined and which surfaces are to be exposed.

**2** **Setting the fence.** With the saw turned off, use a piece of scrap lumber—the same thickness as the boards you will join—to set the fence position. Holding the piece of scrap wood against the fence, move the fence so that, as best your eye can judge, the center of the board's edge lines up with the center of one of the cutters. (The board will be positioned more precisely later.) The center of a cutter is at a point halfway along the sloping line between the bottom of the middle groove and the top of the middle tongue (*inset*).

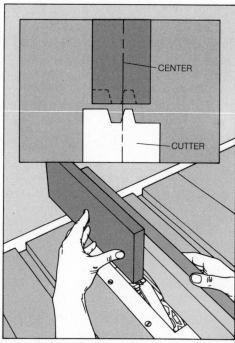

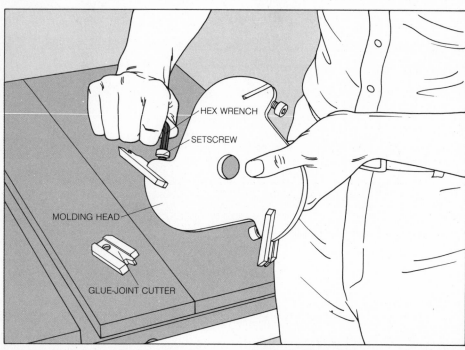

**3** **Bracing for the cut with a featherboard.** Use a featherboard to hold the work against the fence while you push it over the cutters. To make a featherboard, miter the end of a 16-inch-long 2-by-4 at a 45° angle, then cut saw kerfs ⅛ inch apart and roughly 5 inches deep in that end. Before you cut the glue joint, sandwich a scrap of wood—the same thickness as the work—between the featherboard and the fence. Clamp the featherboard to the table, and brace it with a 2-by-4 clamped at a right angle. Adjust the featherboard and the brace so that the scrap moves smoothly forward but will not move backward.

Turn on the saw, run two test scraps over the blades and fit the pieces together. If the faces of the board are not flush, measure the deviation and move the fence half that distance in the direction that will make the boards fit perfectly.

In order to edge two boards that you will actually join, cut the first board with its marked top face against the fence, then run the matching board over the cutters with its unmarked bottom face against the fence. Be sure to begin both cuts at matching ends of the boards.

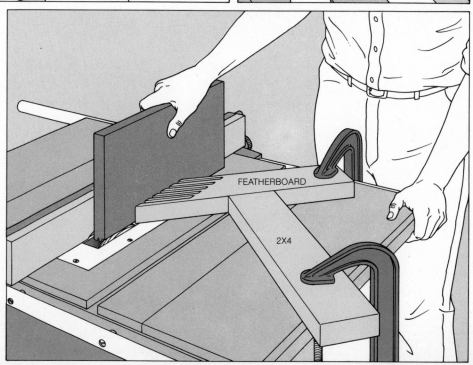

# Two Rigid Corner Joints

A strategic combination of dado and rabbet cuts gives strength to a corner joint by increasing its glue area while locking the joint in every direction but one. A half-blind lock joint (right) and a mitered lock joint (page 51) have the added advantage of hiding the end grain of the boards they join: The half-blind joint is invisible from the front, and the mitered lock joint masks the end grain from both the front and the side.

The half-blind joint is a favorite for attaching drawer fronts, since the joint is hidden from view and resists being pulled apart as the drawer is opened. The mitered lock joint is better than the half-blind joint for corners visible from two sides, and it may be used where a dovetail's strength (page 54) is not needed.

Either kind of lock joint demands precision craftsmanship, but the half-blind joint is the easier of the two. Make sure the boards to be joined are straight, smooth, and squarely cut. Mark each face and edge so that you can keep track of the final positions.

Both joints are started with a wide edge dado that becomes the reference point for all subsequent cuts. Mark the position of each cut as the work progresses and adjust the saw carefully, always testing with scrap pieces the same thickness as the work. Check a finished dado with a rule and with the piece that will fit into it; it may take more than one pass to reach the full depth needed.

**2 Cutting the wide edge dado.** Install a dado head on the table saw, setting it to cut the wide edge dado. The height of the blade should be set to match the thickness of a side piece (right, top). Set the saw fence the same distance from the inside blade as the tongue is wide. To check the setting, mark the position of the edge dado on the front piece, and make sure positions of the blade and the fence match the marks you have made. To make the cut, use a tenoning jig—a purchased metal one that runs in the miter-gauge groove (right) or a wooden one you make to run along the saw fence (inset). To make the wooden jig, screw two pieces of ¾-inch plywood to a spacer the same thickness as the fence. Add a thin strip of wood along one edge of the jig; it will help hold the piece in place while it is being cut.

## Plotting the Cuts for a Half-Blind Lock Joint

**1 Mapping the joint.** On a piece of paper or scrap wood, make a full-scale drawing of the joint; number the cuts (inset). This will help you to visualize how the joint is going to work in the finished product.

Mark the width and the depth of the two dadoes. The width of the tongue that covers the front of the joint should match the width of the tongue that fits in the inside dado. You can vary dimensions, however, to suit the thickness and kind of wood you are using; the dimensions given below are for two pieces of ¾-inch plywood. For solid wood, the tongues should be one fourth to one third the total thickness of the board.

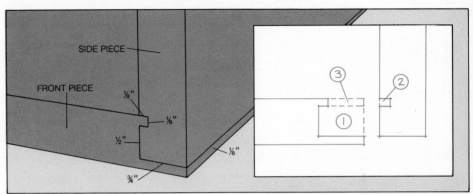

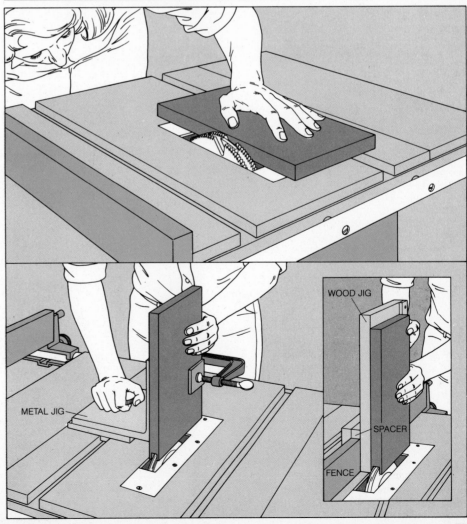

**3** **Cutting the second dado.** Stand the front piece on edge and butt the side piece against it, aligning the inside surface of the front tongue with the end of the side piece. Mark where the rear tongue meets the side piece *(below, left)*; this is the location for the second dado cut.

Adjust the saw blade to the correct width and height for the second dado cut. For a joint in

¾-inch plywood, use a standard blade, which makes a ⅛-inch kerf; in thicker plywood or in solid wood, use two dado blades without chippers. Set the blade height to equal the planned depth of the dado (in this example, ⅛ inch), and use the penciled dado marks to set the fence position. Run a test piece of wood, adjust the blade as needed and, in the side piece, make the second dado cut *(below, right)*.

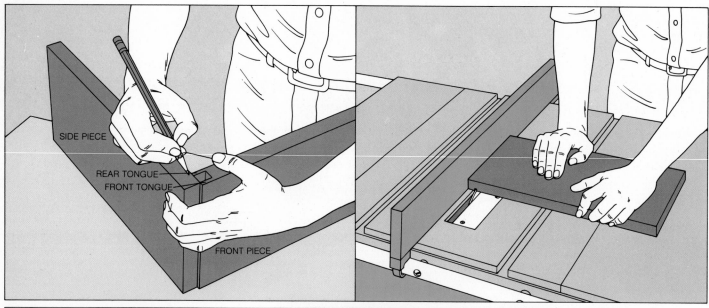

**4** **Trimming the rear tongue.** Stand the front piece on edge and hold the edge of the side piece at a right angle to it, lining up the second dado with the rear tongue and aligning the inside face of the side piece with the bottom surface of the first dado. When all four surfaces are in alignment, insert a pencil in the second dado and make a mark at the point where its bottom surface meets the rear tongue *(above)*. This mark is the trim line for the rear tongue.

To set up the saw for this cut, add an auxiliary wooden fence *(page 47)* to the metal fence of the table saw, leaving a space of about ¼ inch between the auxiliary fence and the tabletop. Use a standard blade, and adjust the position of the fence so that the outer tips of the blade are lined up with the outer edge of the pencil line—the edge that is closest to the fence. Raise the blade slightly and make a test cut. Adjust the position if necessary. When the saw

setting is perfect, trim down the tongue *(above, right)*. Waste wood should slide out of the way in the ¼-inch opening below the auxiliary fence.

When the cuts for the joints at both ends of the front piece have been completed, assemble the joint. First apply yellow glue to all of the interlocking surfaces. Clamp each of the joints with a bar clamp or a pipe clamp, and then wipe away the excess glue *(inset)*.

## A Mitered Joint
## with a Hidden Lock

**1** **Plotting the joint.** Diagram the cuts for the mitered lock joint as for the half-blind lock joint *(page 49, Step 1)*. The two joints use similar cuts, but the mitered lock joint has an additional rabbet cut *(No. 3, inset)* and two bevel cuts *(No. 5 and No. 6)*. Note the depth and the width of the wide dado cut and the rabbet cut *(No. 1 and No. 3)* on the diagram, as well as the depth and width of the narrow dado cut *(No. 2)*. The dimensions shown at right are for two pieces of ¾-inch plywood.

Make the wide dado cut *(No. 1)* with the dado head of the table saw set as for the similar cut in the half-blind lock joint *(page 49, Step 2)*.

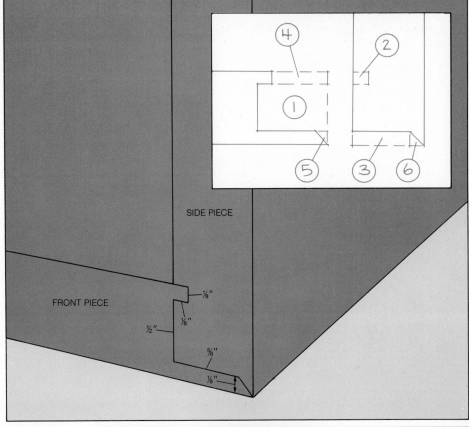

**2** **Cutting the second dado.** Mark the position of the narrow dado in the side piece *(No. 2)* by butting together the edges of the two pieces as for the half-blind lock joint *(opposite, Step 3)*, but position the end of the side piece flush with the outside face of the front piece. Set the blade to the correct width and height, then use the front piece to position the fence: Hold the piece · against the fence, and move both fence and board until the outer tips of the blade are flush with the face of the front piece. Remove the front piece, make a test cut, then cut the dado in the side piece *(opposite, Step 3)*.

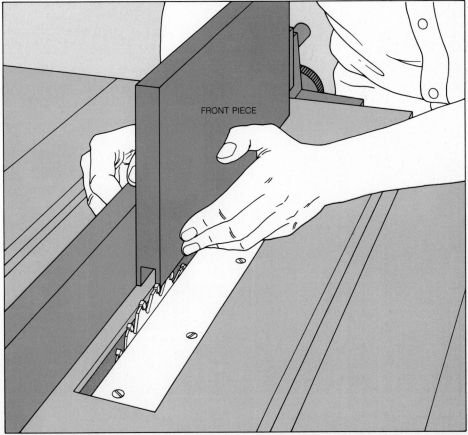

**3 Cutting the rabbet.** To mark the position of the rabbet cut on the edge of the side piece, butt the edge of the front piece against the inside face of the side piece (*below, left*), and extend the line of the inside edge of the front tongue down the edge of the side piece. Add an auxiliary fence (*page 50, Step 4*), leaving a ½-inch space between its lower edge and the table. Adjust the fence so that the outer tips of the saw blade align with the outer edge of the pencil line. Set the blade for the depth of cut on the diagram. Make a test cut and, when the saw is set precisely, cut the rabbet (*below, right*). If the rabbet is more than ⅛ inch wide, snap off the waste wood after the cut is completed.

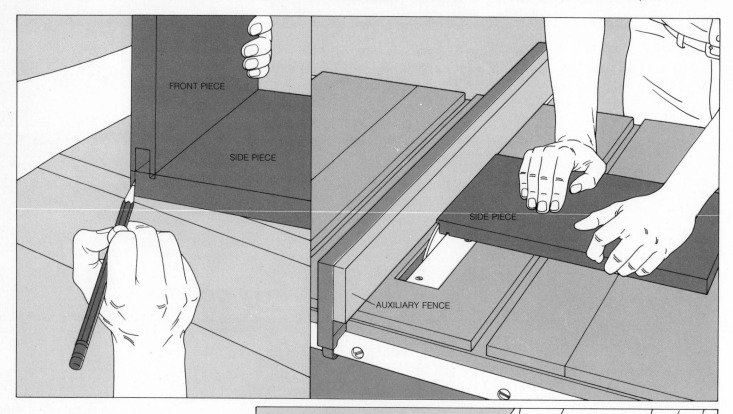

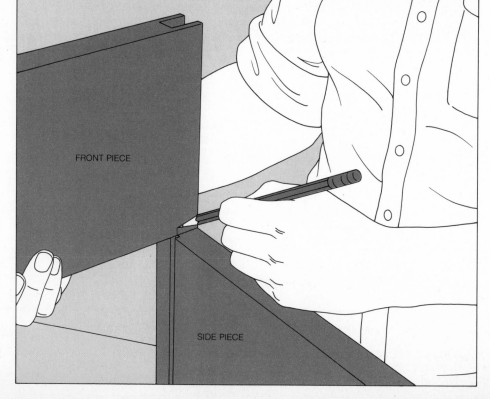

**4 Trimming the rear tongue.** Rest the side piece on edge and hold the front piece above it, aligning the inside face of the front piece with the narrow dado in the side piece. Mark a line where the bottom of the dado meets the face of the front piece. Place the front piece against the auxiliary fence, and move both fence and front piece toward the blade until the outer tips of the blade are aligned with the outer edge of the pencil mark. Make a test cut and then, when the setting is perfect, trim down the rear tongue (*page 50, Step 4*).

**5** **Making the first bevel cut.** If the saw blade ordinarily tilts toward the fence when it is set for a bevel cut, move the rip fence to the other side of the blade. Set the blade for a 45° bevel, and adjust its height to ¼ inch above the tabletop.

Rest the front piece, outside face down, on the far side of the blade, with the rear tongue against the auxiliary fence. Sighting along the tabletop, adjust the fence so that the angle formed by the blade and the tabletop lines up with the outer

edge of the front tongue (*inset*). Make a test cut in scrap wood, to be certain that only the triangular tip of the tongue is removed, and that it is removed cleanly to form a 45° bevel. When the setting is perfect, cut the bevel.

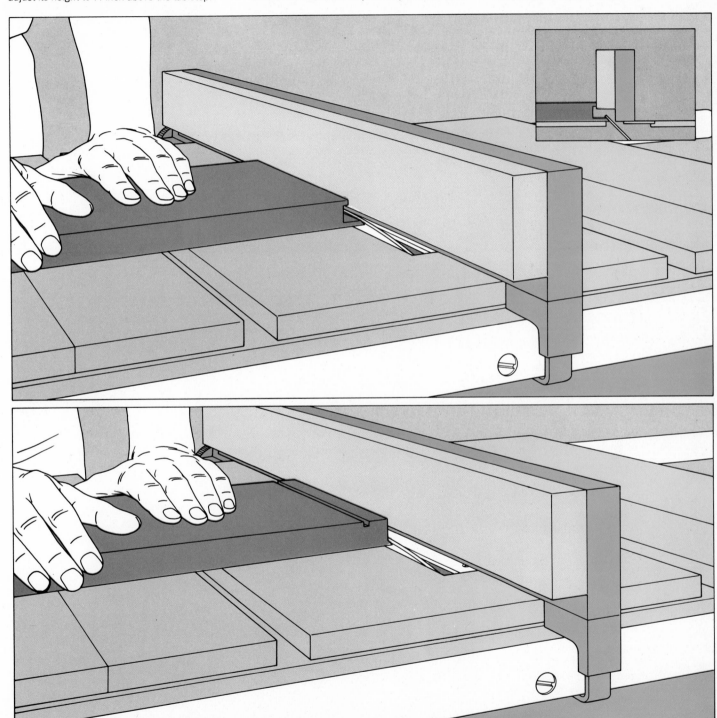

**6** **Cutting the second bevel.** Readjust the fence, but not the blade, for the second bevel cut. Rest the side piece, outside face down, on the far side of the blade; move the fence until it butts against the rabbeted end of the side piece. Ad-

just the side piece and fence in tandem until the blade is aligned to cut a 45° angle in the small tongue at the end of the rabbet. Make a test cut in a piece of scrap wood and then, when the setting is perfect, cut the bevel.

Cut a second joint at the opposite end of the front piece; this joint should be the mirror image of the first one. Then glue and clamp the two joints, using the same procedure as for the half-blind lock joint (*page 50, Step 4*).

# A Hand-cut Joint with Interlocking Tails

The interlocking parts of a dovetail joint are a triumph of the woodworker's art. Often used for decorative effect at the corners of boxes or cabinets, dovetails are equally useful hidden away on the sides of drawers, since they are among the strongest of corner joints. Although uniform dovetails can be made quickly with a router *(page 60)*, the more time-consuming handwork permits you to make a wider variety of sizes and shapes as well as to demonstrate your skill with a number of tools and techniques.

A fine-toothed, straight-cutting saw and sharp wood chisels are the main tools needed for cutting dovetails. A dovetail saw, equipped with tiny teeth that have very little set—deflection from the line of the blade—is best for making the smooth, accurate cuts required. You should also have several chisels of different widths, to allow you to cut with the widest chisel that will fit into a tight space without breaking the corners of the delicate tails and sockets. Chisels with beveled sides allow cutting into the corners of angled sockets.

Clean, well-fitting joints begin with accurate measuring and marking. If your marking gauge has a rounded scribing point, it may scrape rather than cut a line. File its scriber to a knifelike point, thus ensuring a thin, straight mark unaffected by any surface irregularities of the wood. Use a sharp pencil to mark other lines, and further ensure accuracy by always cutting along the side of a line toward the waste wood you are removing. You can always shave away a bit of wood to make a tight joint fit better, but there is no good way of adding wood to a loose joint. If your saw wanders off a line when you are cutting a tail, finish the cut in a straight line. Absolute accuracy is not essential in cutting tails. In cutting the sockets to fit the tails, however, there is no margin for error.

Since most dovetail joints are part of a rectangular assembly, you will cut and fit four joints before gluing and clamping any of them. Mark the matching pieces of each joint before you begin cutting, for easy identification at later stages. If your plan calls for a bottom or a back that will be set in a groove, cut the groove after cutting the joints, and add the bottom or back when you glue the unit together.

## Two Versions of a Classic Connection

**Through and lap dovetail joints.** The simplest and strongest dovetail joint is the through dovetail *(top right)*, which exposes end grain on both sides of the joint. Here the interlocking of the angled tails with the narrower pins on the socket piece *(inset)* gives the joint great holding power. The angle of these tails is 80° in softwoods, 83° in hardwoods. The pins are cut at least ¼ inch wide on their narrow sides and are spaced no more than 3 inches apart center to center.

In the lap dovetail *(bottom right)*, the end grain of the tail piece is hidden by closed sockets. The tails, cut at least ¼ inch shorter than the thickness of the socket piece, are otherwise identical with those in the through dovetail.

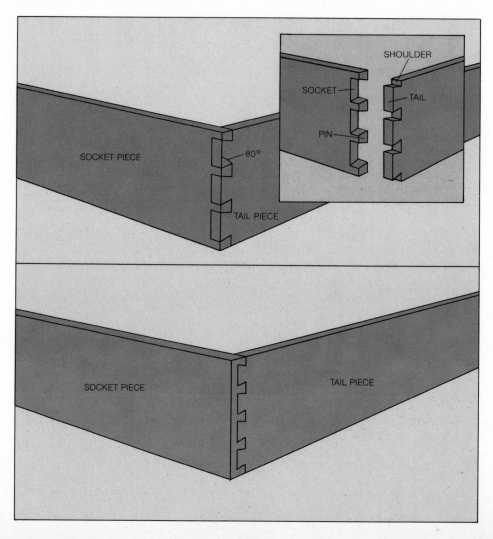

# Cutting a Through Dovetail

**1** **Marking thickness for tails and pins.** Set a marking gauge to match the thickness of the socket piece, and use it to scribe a line on all sides of the end of the tail piece. Then set the marking gauge to the thickness of the tail piece, and scribe a line on both sides of the matching end of the socket piece.

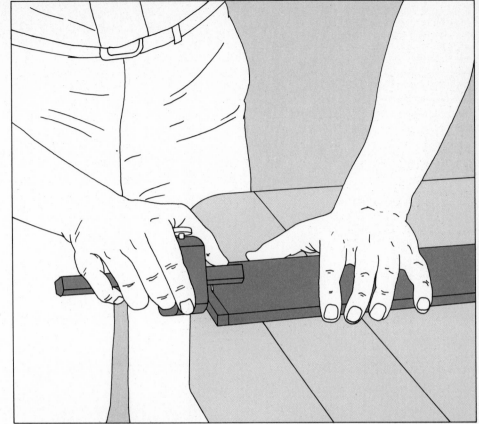

**2** **Laying out the tails.** Lay out the positions of the tails with squared lines across the end of the tail piece; then use a T bevel, set to the desired angle, to extend the lines along the side of the tail piece to the marking-gauge line. In laying out the tails, first establish the outer corners by marking two lines across the end of the tail piece; position each line so that its distance from the corners is equal to half the thickness of the socket piece. Divide the space between these two lines into equal sections for the tails, leaving at least ¼ inch for pins between adjacent tails.

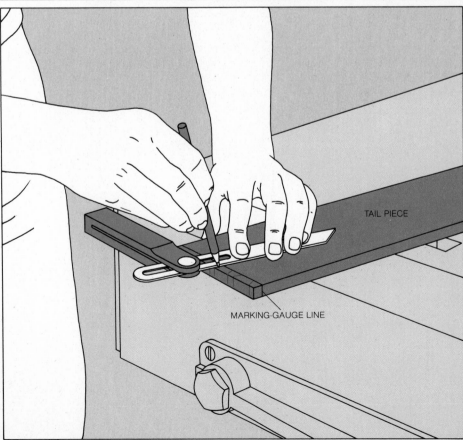

TAIL PIECE

MARKING-GAUGE LINE

**3** **Cutting the tails and shoulders.** Clamp the tail piece in a vise so that the lines on one side of each tail are exactly vertical *(top right)*, and use a dovetail saw to cut along each vertical line down to the marking-gauge line. Then change the position of the tail piece in the vise so that the remaining lines are vertical, and cut along each of these lines in the same way.

Reposition the tail piece in the vise so that the marking-gauge line is vertical *(bottom right)*, and use the dovetail saw to cut along the marking-gauge line from the edge of the piece to the cut at the base of the first tail. Reclamp the piece with the opposite edge up, and cut the other shoulder in the same way.

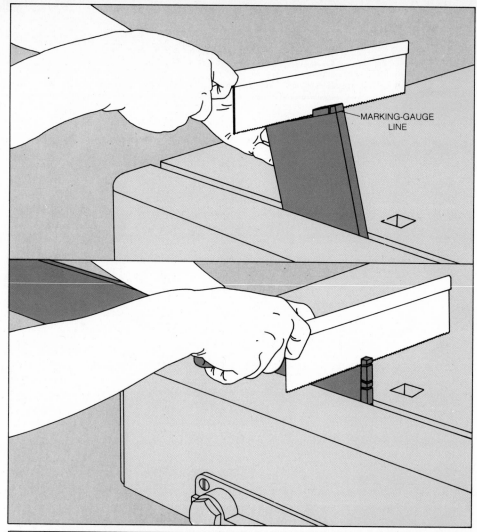

MARKING-GAUGE
LINE

**4** **Cutting out the waste.** Clamp the tail piece vertically in the vise and use a coping saw to cut out as much of the waste wood between the tails as possible. Begin each cut in a saw kerf beside one tail, and cut to the kerf beside the adjacent tail, using extreme caution to avoid sawing below the marking-gauge line.

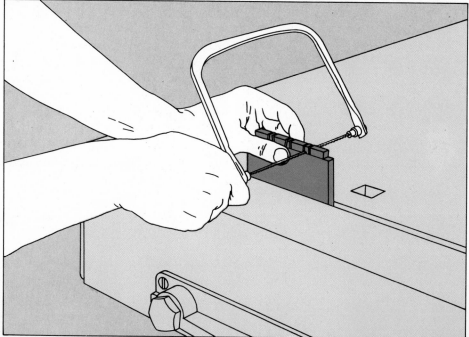

**5** **Chiseling out the waste.** Clamp the tail piece on top of scrap wood on a flat work surface, and use a sharp chisel to cut away the remaining waste between the tails. Begin chiseling across the grain, positioning the chisel edge on the marking-gauge line, bevel facing out, and tapping it lightly with a mallet. Then use the chisel to cut along the grain from the end of the tail piece, removing a thin shaving down to the chisel cut at the marking-gauge line. Cut across and along the grain about half the width of the board, then chisel out waste between the other tails in the same way. Turn the tail piece over and re-clamp it, then chisel out the waste from that side until all the spaces between the tails are clear.

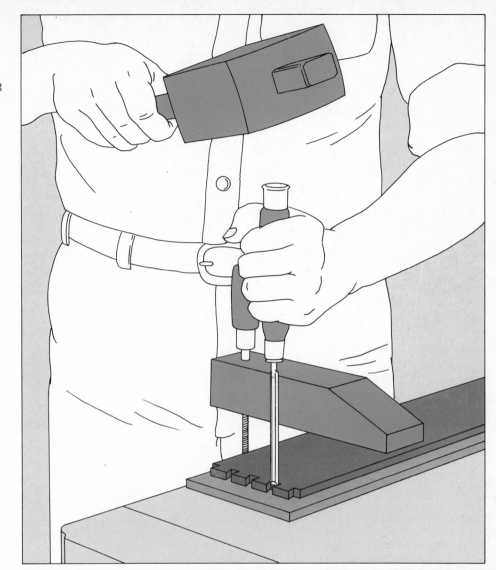

**6** **Marking the socket piece.** Clamp the socket piece in a vise so that the amount exposed above the work surface is equal to the thickness of a support block of scrap wood. Position the tail piece so that the tails are aligned with the end of the socket piece and the other end is resting on the scrap block. Hold the tail piece firmly against the socket piece, and use a sharp pencil to trace the outline of the tails on the end of the socket piece. Then use a try square to continue the lines down each side of the socket piece to the marking-gauge line.

Use a dovetail saw to cut along the marked lines down to the marking-gauge line, then use a coping saw to cut away as much of the waste as possible. Use a chisel and a mallet to cut out the remaining waste from each of the sockets.

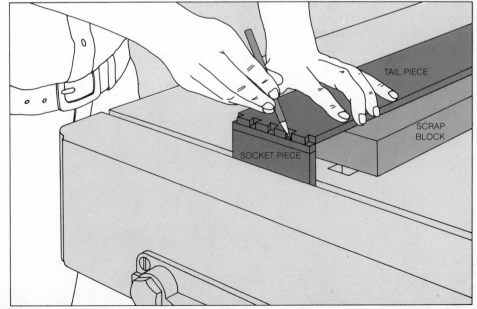

TAIL PIECE

SCRAP BLOCK

SOCKET PIECE

**7 Fitting the joint.** Clamp the socket piece vertically in the vise, position the tails in the sockets, and tap the tail piece lightly with a mallet to test the fit of the joint; use scrap wood on top of the tail piece to distribute the pressure evenly. There should be some friction in the joint, but if it is too tight to be seated with light tapping, disassemble it and use a chisel to slice thin shavings from the sides of the tails.

After cutting and fitting all the joints of a unit, cover the contacting surfaces of each joint with a thin coat of yellow glue. Then put the unit together and use bar clamps to apply light tension across the tail pieces *(inset)*.

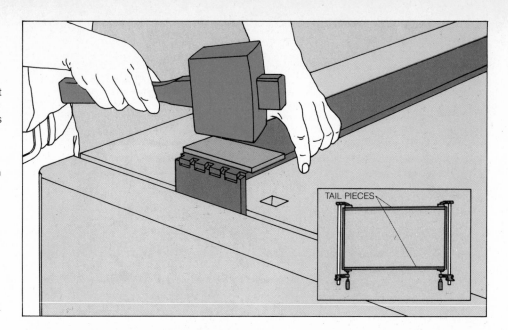

TAIL PIECES

## Cutting a Lap Dovetail

**1 Cutting the sockets.** After cutting a tail piece with tails shorter than the thickness of the socket piece *(pages 55-57, Steps 1-5)*, mark the outline of the tails on the end of the socket piece *(page 57, Step 6)*. Then use a try square to continue the lines down the inside of the socket piece to the marking-gauge line. With a dovetail saw, cut the sides of each socket, holding the saw at an angle so that it follows the angled line on the end of the socket piece as well as the straight line on the side *(top right)*.

Use the dovetail saw to cut some of the waste from the socket by cutting at an angle from the center of the socket to each of the previous cuts *(bottom right)*. Be certain that you avoid cutting into the marking-gauge line.

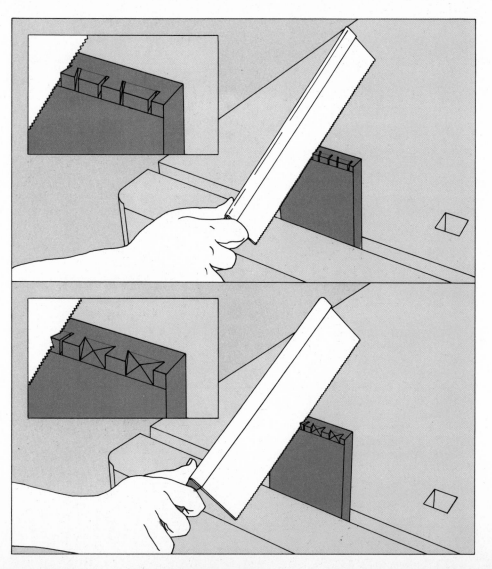

**2** **Chiseling out the sockets.** Position a sharp chisel, flat side down, on the marking-gauge line and tap it lightly with a mallet (*below, top*). Then position the chisel inside the socket and tap it lightly so that you remove a thin shaving (*below, bottom*). Continue removing shavings, alternately cutting across and along the grain, until you have cleared the waste from the center of the socket. Avoid chiseling into the angled corners of the socket, to keep from breaking the edges of the pins. Chisel out the centers of the remaining sockets in the same way.

**3** **Clearing out the corners.** Use a narrow chisel with beveled sides to undercut the waste in the corners of each socket. Cut with hand pressure only, if possible; otherwise, tap the chisel lightly with the mallet. Cut alternately across and along the grain until you have cleared all the waste out of the sockets. Then assemble the joint as in Step 7, page 58.

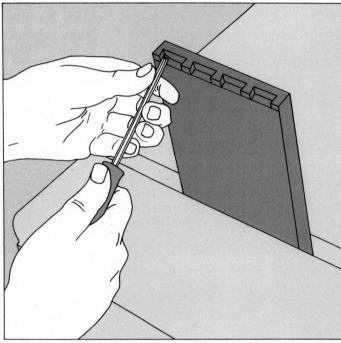

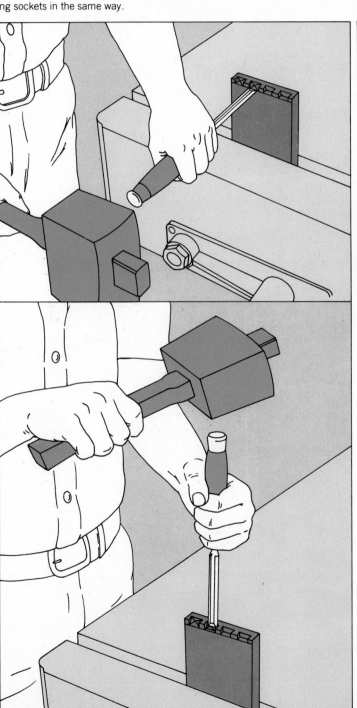

# Dovetails Made by the Dozen

For projects that require large numbers of dovetail joints, a time-saving alternative to hand cutting *(page 54)* is the use of a router guided by a special device called a dovetail template. The template makes it possible to shape both sides of a simple dovetail joint simultaneously, carving out tails and pins of uniform size. If you use machine-made dovetails, the joints will be less decorative but only slightly less strong than the alternating thick and thin tails and pins of hand-cut joints.

With its many-tongued template and numerous adjustments, the dovetailing device looks complicated to use, but in fact it is not. The adjustments clamp two boards at right angles to each other against the top and side of the metal base; the template is lowered against them to guide the router. Moving in and out between the tongues, the router cuts tails in one board and matching sockets in the other. Once the device and the router are aligned, the work goes quickly and easily on corner after corner.

The best way to set up the device is to cut a test joint on scrap lumber the same thickness and width as the two pieces to be joined. The test joint should fit snugly, the two pieces meeting flush at the corners and the tails completely seated in the sockets. If the joint is too loose, you can correct it by slightly increasing the depth setting of the router. If the joint is too tight to fit together when tapped lightly with a mallet, decrease the router's depth setting. If the tails fall above or below the surface of the sockets, adjust the position of the template: For sockets that are too shallow, move the template backward by turning the adjusting nuts clockwise; for overly deep sockets, turn the adjusting nuts counterclockwise, bringing the template forward.

The orientation of the router during the cut can also affect the depth and snugness of the joint. While you are cutting test joints, note the position of the router handles with relation to the work; when you achieve a good fit, make all subsequent cuts with the router handles in this position. When the test joint is perfect, do not change the adjustments until you have finished cutting all the dovetails. But do not discard the test joint, for if you plan to repeat joints of the same dimensions later, you can use the test joint to reset the bit depth on the router.

By changing the size of the router bit and the template, you can make dovetails of several sizes. The most common dovetails are ½ inch or ¼ inch wide across the widest part of the tail. The broader ones are generally used for drawers and cabinets, the narrower for small boxes.

Whatever the size of the dovetails, the cutting positions for making the joint are always the same. The tail piece is always vertical against the front of the base, the socket piece horizontal against the top of the base. If the finished joint will be exposed, you can sometimes improve its appearance by making slight adjustments in the total width of the joint so that it begins and ends on a half pin. To achieve this effect, make the final tail half as wide as the distance between the tips of the template tongues.

**Flush and rabbeted dovetail joints.** When assembled, the tail and socket pieces of a router-cut dovetail joint look much like those of a hand-cut dovetail except that the tails and pins are identical in size *(below, top)*. The hidden ends of the tails and sockets are rounded, however, and the tail cuts in the socket piece usually do not extend through the wood's full thickness *(inset)*.

When the joint includes a lip, as on a drawer front *(below, bottom)*, the socket piece can be cut first and rabbeted after cutting. But it is simpler to rabbet it beforehand and slip a grooved gauge block *(inset)* over the rabbeted lip to position the socket piece properly against the template base. The preliminary setup for a rabbeted dovetail is identical with that of a flush dovetail except for the position of the socket piece on top of the base. Also, when the drawer lip is rabbeted first, the two pieces must be cut separately rather than simultaneously.

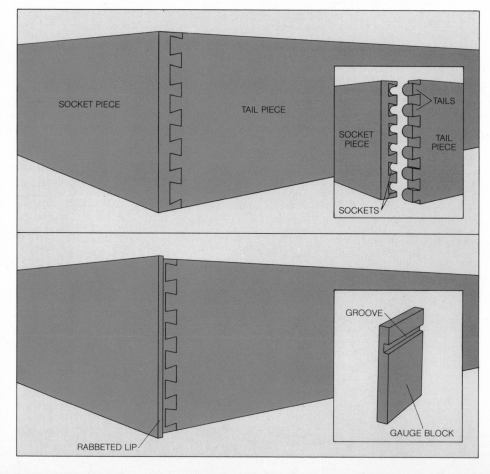

## Assembling the Template and Router

**Setting up a template and router.** A dovetail template device (*below, left*) and a specially fitted router (*below, right*) together make short work of cutting the two parts of an interlocking dovetail joint. The template device is shown here mounted on a 2-by-8 clamped to the top of a worktable, but it could be mounted directly on the work surface. The device consists of a channel-shaped base, above which lies the actual template. Two knobs, one on each template

bracket, adjust the template's height, and two nuts behind the brackets (*inset*) move the template forward or backward for fine tuning; on some models, the spacers for this horizontal adjustment can be relocated on the outside of the bracket and used in lieu of a gauge block (*opposite, bottom inset*) to cut rabbeted dovetails.

The two boards being cut are held by bar clamps against the top and front of the base; on most

models, the clamps can be adjusted so that they will fit boards up to 13¼ inches wide and 1¼ inches thick. The boards are butted against stop screws on the top and front of the base; the screws are offset to the precise distance required to bring the finished joint into alignment. The router base is fitted with a guide bushing that follows the exact contours of the template. And the special dovetail bit is tapered to cut precisely angled tails and sockets.

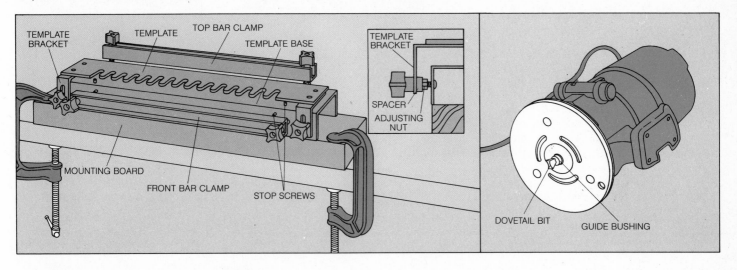

## Routing to Make a Flush Dovetail

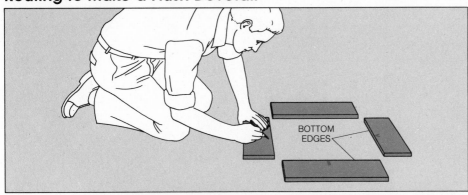

**1 Marking the pieces.** Lay the pieces on a flat surface in the order they will assume when assembled, with their bottom edges toward each other and their inside faces up. Mark the front piece with the letter A, then mark the remaining pieces B through D, moving clockwise. Place each mark near the bottom edge of the piece, to help orient each piece in the dovetail template. The bottom edges will always abut the stop screws, and the inside faces will always face away from the template base.

**2 Setting up the first piece.** Place the side piece marked D inside the front bar clamp at the right side of the template base, with its bottom edge against the stop screw. Slide the piece up until its end is about ¼ inch above the surface of the template base. Tighten the front bar clamp.

**3** **Setting up the second piece.** Slide the front piece, marked A, under the top bar clamp at the right side of the template base, bottom edge against the stop screw and end butted squarely against the side of piece D. Tighten the top bar clamp. Then loosen the front bar clamp slightly, and slide piece D up until its end is flush with the top surface of piece A. Lower the template over the two pieces, and fasten it in position with the locking knobs on the base *(inset)*.

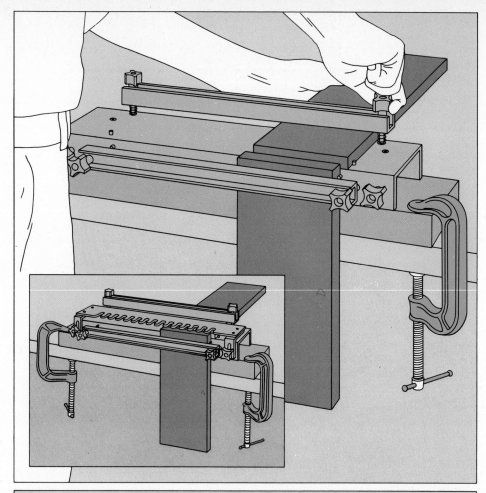

**4** **Routing the outer edge.** Beginning at the right side of the template base, position the guide bushing of the router against the slotted template; switch on the router, and begin moving it from right to left. Move the router straight across the edge of the piece held by the front clamp, touching each tongue of the slotted template with the guide bushing as the router passes it.

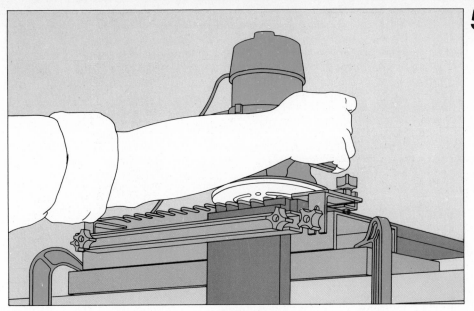

**5** **Completing the joint.** Starting at the left side of the two pieces, move the router slowly to the right, using the guide bushing to follow the contours of the template tongues. When the cut is complete, switch off the router and allow it to come to a stop; then withdraw the router from the template, pulling it directly toward you. Remove the two pieces from the fixture, and clean away any splinters around the tails and sockets with a utility knife.

Cut the other side of the front piece, marked A, in the same way, matching it with the side piece marked B, but for this cut clamp the assembly against the left side of the template base. Repeat the same procedures with the back piece, marked C, and the uncut ends of the two side pieces. Assemble the joints as you would hand-cut dovetails (*page 58, Step 7*).

## Adjusting the Template for a Rabbeted Lip

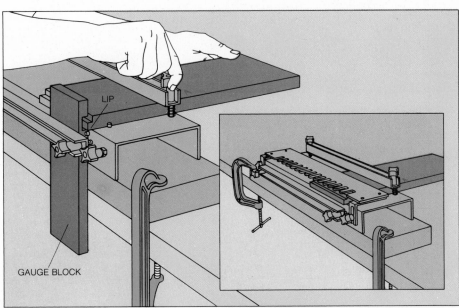

**1** **Cutting the sockets.** Use a grooved gauge block to position a lipped drawer front atop the dovetail base. Clamp the block against the front of the base, lining up the bottom of the groove with the top of the base; then slide the lipped drawer front into the groove until the offset edge meets the side of the block. Tighten the top clamp, then remove the gauge block. Lower the dovetail template against the drawer front (*inset*) and use the router to cut sockets in the offset edge, following the tongues of the template with the guide bushing as in Step 5.

**2** **Cutting the tails.** Clamp a piece of scrap wood the same thickness as the drawer front against the top of the template base, and position the side piece against it as in Step 3, opposite. Lower the template, and cut the tails on the side piece as in Steps 4 and 5.

Repeat Steps 1 and 2 at the opposite edge of the drawer first and on the other side piece, clamping the work to the left side of the template base. Cut the joints for the drawer back as for an ordinary flush dovetail joint (*Steps 1-5*).

# The Box Joint: A Fast Dovetail

Before plastics and cardboard became preferred for packaging, many products—ranging from dried figs to dried codfish—were sold in inexpensive pine boxes. The popularity of the quickly made, machine-cut box joint dates from that period. Its straight-sided fingers and slots may lack the holding power of the dovetail joint, with its splayed pins and tails, but the box joint still is surprisingly strong. The many fingers along each side of the joint add up to a gluing surface as much as three times as long as the joint.

Box joints are cut on a table saw in a series of simple, purely mechanical actions. But the jig used to guide the cut must be constructed and positioned with care, and then checked in operation on scrap wood, to be sure the joint pieces meet precisely. Also, the size and location of the fingers should be determined in advance. For symmetry, a complete finger should fall at each end of the joint.

The cutting is done with a dado head fitted with enough chippers between the blades to bring the head to the desired finger width. The head should be set to cut about 1/16 inch higher than the thickness of the wood. A cut of this depth will produce a joint whose fingers extend slightly above the surface of the adjoining piece, but the unevenness is sanded away after completing the joint.

When you have cut all four corners of the box, glue and clamp each corner in both directions, using small bar clamps. If you use blocks of scrap wood to protect the wood surface from clamp mars, cut a rabbet in the part of each block that laps over the slightly protruding fingers.

**A box joint and its jig.** Square-cut fingers and slots on the ends of matching boards interlock to form a box joint (*below, left*). The width of the fingers and slots—which are identical in size—usually is about 1/8 to 1/2 inch less than the thickness of the wood being joined. The slots are cut with the aid of a special jig (*below, right*) attached to the miter gauge of a table saw. The jig is a piece of 3/4-inch plywood, 4 inches high and equal in length to the distance from the miter gauge to about 8 inches past the dado head. A hardwood guide pin, the same thickness as a finger of the joint, is attached to the front of the jig, slightly off center. It is held in a slot on the bottom of the jig by a countersunk screw driven through the bottom of the pin into the plywood. The slot is cut with the dado head, set for the dimensions of the slots of the joint.

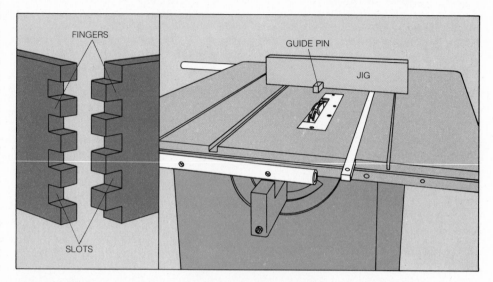

FINGERS

SLOTS

GUIDE PIN

JIG

## Cutting Serrated Ends with a Dado Head

DADO HEAD

SPACER BLOCK

GUIDE PIN

**1** **Attaching the jig.** Hold the jig, with its guide pin in place, against the face of the miter gauge, and move the miter gauge forward until the front of the jig nearly touches the teeth of the dado head. Put a wooden spacer block, the same thickness as the guide pin, against the side of the dado head, and move the jig sideways until the guide pin presses the block snug against the dado head. Holding the jig in this position, attach it to the miter gauge with wood screws.

**2** **Making the first slot.** Hold the inside face of the first board firmly against the jig, with one long edge butted against the guide pin. Switch on the saw, and push the jig and board slowly across the dado head, cutting a slot through both the board and the jig. Switch off the saw and wait for it to stop, then return the jig to its starting position.

**3** **Cutting the remaining slots.** Reposition the board by slipping the first slot (*Step 2*) over the guide pin. Hold the board firmly against the jig, and cut another slot. Cut each subsequent slot by repositioning each newly cut slot over the guide pin in the same manner.

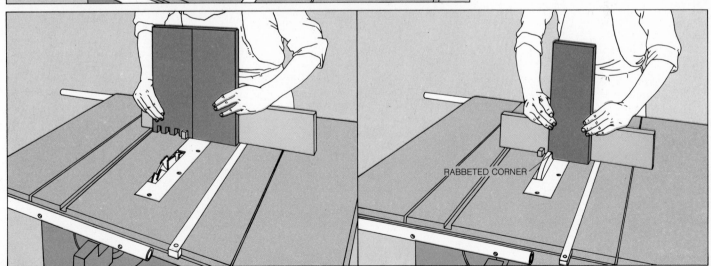

RABBETED CORNER

**4** **Cutting the matching board.** Position the first board so that its outside face is against the jig and the first slot fits over the guide pin. Butt the matching board up against it, putting the inside face against the jig (*above, left*). Hold the matching board firmly against the jig, and remove the first board. Then push the matching board across the dado head, so that a rabbet is cut at the corner (*above, right*). Slip the rabbet over the guide pin and continue cutting additional slots across the board, as in Step 3, ending with a rabbet in the opposite corner.

# Mortise and Tenon: Elements of a Strong Joint

Mortise-and-tenon joinery is based on a simple premise: Hollow out a space in one piece, and shape a projection on a second piece to fit into it. The connection, as well as being simple, is strong—especially for joints where pressure will be applied perpendicular to the narrow edge of the second piece. It is often found in furniture parts that have cross braces, such as table or chair legs—the legs have the hollowed-out spaces, called mortises, and the cross braces have the projections, called tenons. Variations of this joint bind the frames of many cabinet doors and window sashes.

The general rule in planning a mortise-and-tenon joint is to make the tenon between one third and one half the thickness of the piece from which it projects. A tenon thinner than one third the thickness is likely to be weak, while a tenon wider than half the thickness of the piece may leave the mortise sides too thin.

Although in the planning stage the size of the tenon is considered first, in execution it is the mortise that leads; for if any mistake is made in fashioning the mortise, the tenon can still be shaped to fit. Mortises can be scooped out with a hand drill and a chisel, but power tools make neater holes with less effort. Similarly, tenons can be fashioned with a dovetail saw; but a table saw (or even a band saw) makes faster, cleaner cuts.

An excellent power tool for hollowing mortises is the drill press. It can be fitted with a special accessory, called a mortiser, that has a regular drill bit sheathed in a square cutter. The bit drills a round hole; the cutter trims it to make it square. But even without the mortiser, a drill press can cut a series of holes that are easy to square later with a chisel.

Boards too long for a drill-press table can be mortised with a router. The tool's high-speed cutting action leaves clean sides and a hole that needs less chiseling than drill-press holes.

If neither a drill press nor a router is available, a portable electric drill will suffice. Its only drawback is a lack of built-in accuracy; fitted with a special drill-guide attachment, however, it will produce tolerably straight holes perpendicular to a board edge. Like the router, the portable drill leaves a rounded mortise that must be squared with a chisel. Although squaring the mortise is standard practice, some woodworkers find it easier and faster to round the ends of the tenon instead.

A joint similar to the mortise-and-tenon joint and one also used for the frames of furniture, windows and cabinets is the lap joint. Both adjoining pieces have projecting ends, like tenons, but the cutaway portions are formed in the course of shaping the projections. Lap-joint pieces are cut with the techniques used for tenons.

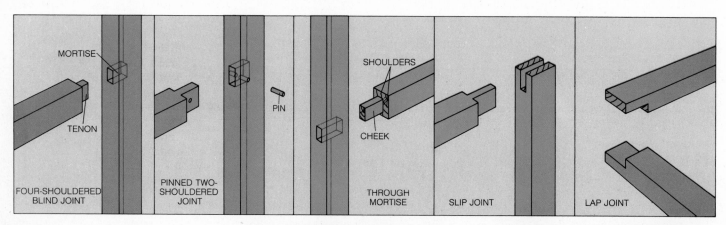

FOUR-SHOULDERED BLIND JOINT · PINNED TWO-SHOULDERED JOINT · PIN · THROUGH MORTISE · SLIP JOINT · LAP JOINT · MORTISE · TENON · SHOULDERS · CHEEK

**Joinery with mortises and tenons.** Mortise-and-tenon joints can take several forms, varying in appearance and strength. When the mortise does not extend through the piece from one side to the other, the joint is called blind. The blind joint shown is called four-shouldered because the tenon is recessed at the top and bottom and on the two sides, or cheeks, so that four shoulders are formed. This joint is useful when one or both pieces are to be carved, since the shoulders can be whittled without exposing the mortise or the tenon. Uncarved, the broad shoulders are useful for covering any scratches or mistakes made in cutting the mortise.

The two-shouldered mortise is slightly stronger than its four-shouldered cousin because its tenon is larger, offering a greater gluing surface. The one shown here is additionally strengthened by a dowel and is called a pinned joint. Any mortise-and-tenon joint can be pinned for added strength. The through mortise has a mortise that penetrates to the far side of the mortise piece and exposes the end grain of the tenon; the joint is decorative when done in tables or chairs and is particularly useful in narrow wood, where a mortise cut only partway through does not provide for a deep enough tenon. The slip joint, often known as an open mortise joint, is found in many chairs and tables; it is faster to make than a true mortise joint. The lap joint is quicker still; it consists of two lapped tenons and no mortise at all. It is commonly used for joining the pieces of cabinet-frame fronts.

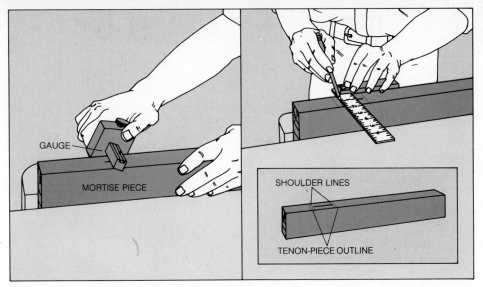

GAUGE

MORTISE PIECE

SHOULDER LINES

TENON-PIECE OUTLINE

## Marking Wood for a Mortise

**Scribing the drilling line.** Set the pin of a marking gauge at the approximate center of the edge of the board; then press the pin into the board, leaving a mark. Rest the gauge against the other side of the board, and make a mark. Repeat the measurements, adjusting the pin until the two marks overlap—this indicates that you have located the exact center of the edge. Draw the gauge down the board, scribing a line slightly shorter than the length of the mortise.

Butt the tenon piece against the marked edge of the mortise piece, and outline where its edges fall. For a four-shouldered joint, measure in from these two lines, and use a try square to mark top and bottom shoulders of equal width on the mortise edge (*near left*).

## Cutting a Mortise with a Drill Press

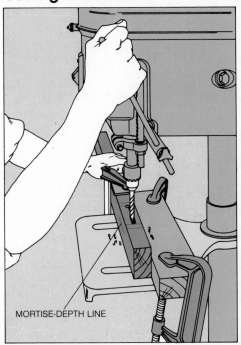

MORTISE-DEPTH LINE

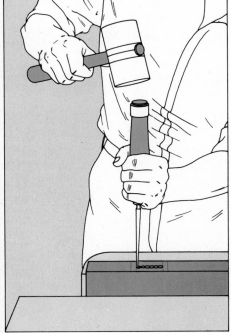

## Drill-Press Safety Rules

The drill press is a precision drilling machine with a small worktable. In addition to following the general precautions for power tools listed on page 9, observe these safety rules:
☐ Clamp the stock to the table before you begin drilling.
☐ When making a deep hole, raise the bit frequently to clean out fragments of waste wood.
☐ Keep the table clean.
☐ Use only bits that are designed for the drill press, not auger bits, which are not made for high-speed use.
☐ Turn off the machine if the bit begins to bind.

**1 Drilling out the cavity.** Using a drill bit the same width as the planned mortise, bore a row of holes down the scribed mortise line. To adjust the drill, first mark the planned depth of the mortise on the board face and lower the cutting edge of the bit to that line; lock the depth stop. To adjust the mortise board, move it until the drill tip falls exactly over the mortise line; clamp the board to the table and steady it with a wood block, also clamped to the table.

Drill a hole at one end of the mortise line, just inside the shoulder line, and a similar hole at the other end. Then drill holes in between, overlapping adjacent holes slightly.

**2 Squaring the mortise with a chisel.** Clamp the mortise board in a vise, and use a marking gauge to scribe lines along both sides of the row of holes. At one end of the mortise, position a chisel that has a blade the same width as the mortise. Holding the shaft of the chisel exactly perpendicular, bevel facing the row of holes, tap the chisel with a mallet, squaring the end of the mortise. Repeat this procedure at the other end of the mortise.

Smooth each side of the mortise in the same fashion, positioning the chisel blade so that the beveled edge faces the holes, the chisel shaft so that the cut will be straight down.

# Using a Router to Make a Mortise

**1 Setting up the router guides.** Install a straight bit with a diameter at least half the planned mortise width, and slide an edge guide onto one side of the router. Make the distance between the guide and the bit equal to the width of the planned tenon shoulder; lock the guide in place.

To position the second edge guide, use a piece of scrap wood—the same thickness as the mortise board—as a template. Outline the mortise on the edge of the template, and clamp it in a vise. Slide the second guide onto the router, and place the router over the edge of the template. Butt the first guide against one face of the template, and bring the second guide tight against the opposite face; lock the second guide in place (*inset*). Adjust the router bit to the desired depth of cut, and make a test cut on the edge of the template to check the width of the shoulder. Adjust as necessary. When the width is correct, put the actual mortise board in place.

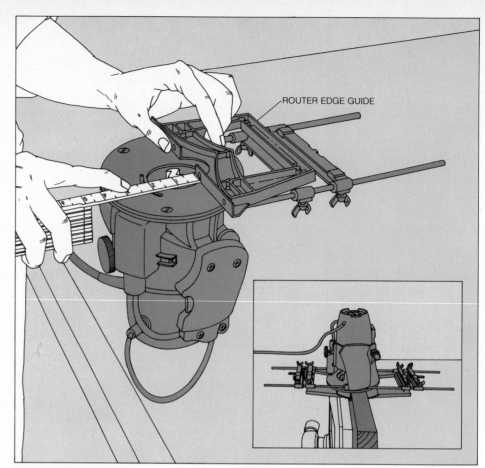

ROUTER EDGE GUIDE

**2 Making the cuts.** Hold the router so that the first edge guide—the one offset from the bit the same distance as the shoulder width—is on the side near you. Tilt the router against the mortise board so that the bit is slightly inside one end of the mortise marks, then turn on the router and slowly lower the bit into the board. Move the router down to the other end of the mortise and back, cutting a groove that barely touches both ends of the mortise. Turn off the router, and wait until the bit stops before lifting it.

Turn the board around and rout the other side of the mortise. Square the ends of the mortise with a chisel as shown in Step 2, page 67.

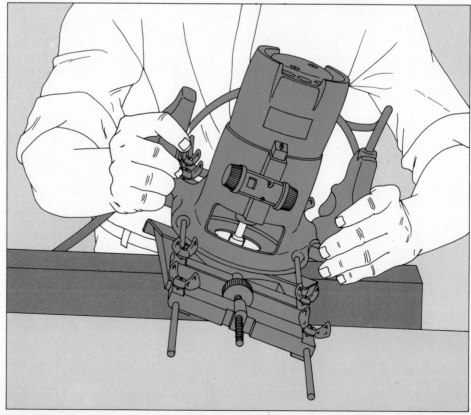

# Shaping the Shoulders of a Matching Tenon

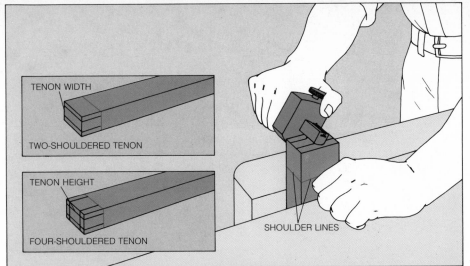

TENON WIDTH

TWO-SHOULDERED TENON

TENON HEIGHT

FOUR-SHOULDERED TENON

SHOULDER LINES

**1 Marking the cutting lines.** With a try square, draw a continuous line around all four sides of the tenon piece, marking the tenon shoulders. Make the tenon ⅛ inch shorter than the depth of the mortise. Using a marking gauge, scribe lines on the end of the tenon piece to mark the width of the tenon, making it the same width as the mortise. Continue these lines down the edge of the board until they meet the shoulder lines (*top inset, left*). If the tenon is to have four shoulders, mark its height by scribing two additional lines, and extend them down to meet the shoulder lines (*bottom inset, left*).

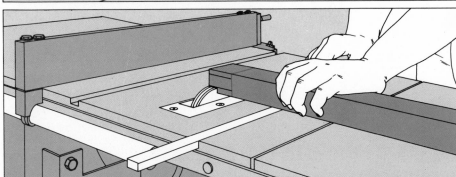

**2 Adjusting the saw-blade height.** Install a dado head on the table saw, and raise the head to a height roughly equal to the width of the tenon shoulder. Then lower it by a half turn of the blade-height crank. Using the miter gauge as a guide, cut a ½-inch rabbet in one side of the tenon; then turn the board over and do the same on the other side. Test the tenon against the mortise. If they do not fit, raise the blade height very slightly and repeat the two cuts until tenon and mortise size match. Keep the blade at this height for the remainder of the tenon cuts.

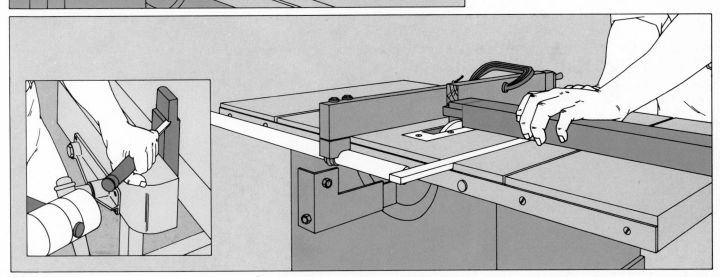

**3 Completing the tenon cut.** Clamp a wooden block to the rip fence, to use as a depth guide in cutting the tenon shoulder. Make the block just long enough to extend from the near end of the fence to a point just short of where the tips of the dado blades will start to cut. Move the fence and the wooden block toward the blades until the distance between the block and the blade edge farthest from the fence is equal to the distance from the shoulder line to the end of the tenon. Lock the fence. Butt the end of the tenon board against the block and, pushing with the miter gauge, cut the shoulder. Bring the board back to the starting point and move it away from the block, so that the next pass will remove an uncut section of wood between the shoulder and the end of the tenon. Continue until the entire tenon side is exposed. Then turn the board over, and repeat these cuts to remove the wood from the other side of the mortise. The fit should be snug but not so tight as to compress grain on the tenon cheeks.

For a four-shouldered tenon, use the same technique, but cut shoulders on all four sides of the tenon board. If you have left the ends of the mortise curved rather than squaring them off, round off the corners of the tenon as well. To do this, clamp the tenon board in a woodworking vise, and chip off the corners with a chisel held flat side down (*inset*). Then hold the chisel in a vertical position, bevel side out, and pare down the sharp corners. Smooth and round the corners with a rasp and a piece of sandpaper.

## Pinning a Mortise and Tenon with a Dowel

**1 Drilling the dowel hole.** Fit a piece of scrap wood, roughly the same thickness as the tenon, into the empty mortise. Install a bit of the desired dowel diameter in the drill press, and set the depth gauge so that it will stop the tip of the bit when it has passed through one side of the mortise and has penetrated at least halfway into the other side. Position the bit above the midpoint of the mortise, slightly closer to the front edge; then drill the hole for the dowel. The piece of scrap wood will prevent the mortise wall from splintering as you drill.

Discard the scrap wood, and insert the tenon in the mortise. Lay both on a worktable, and push a drill bit—the one just used or one of identical size—through the dowel hole until its tip has marked the tenon (*inset*). Remove the bit from the hole, and the tenon from the mortise.

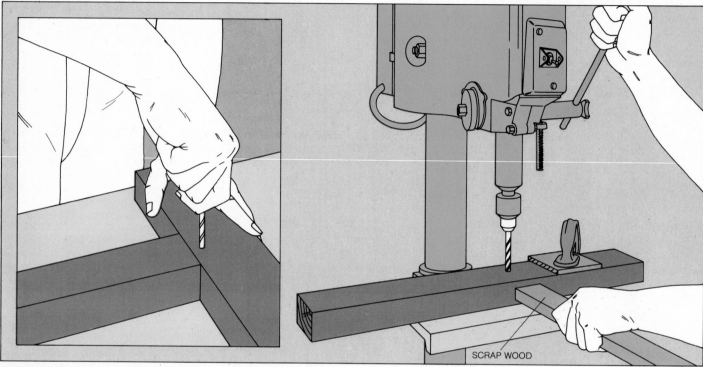

SCRAP WOOD

**2 Shifting the hole mark.** To draw the shoulders tight, make a pencil mark on the tenon about a thumbnail's thickness away from the impression made by the drill-bit tip, in toward the shoulder. Drill a hole in the tenon, identical in size to the one in the mortise, using the second mark as the center. Cut a dowel the same diameter as the hole and ¼ inch longer; chamfer its end.

Spread glue in the mortise and on both the end and the shoulders of the tenon, and fit the pieces together. Spread glue in the dowel hole and on the chamfered end of the dowel, and tap the dowel into the hole. Let the glue set for a day, then trim the dowel flush with the face of the mortise board, using a dovetail saw; finally, sand the dowel end smooth.

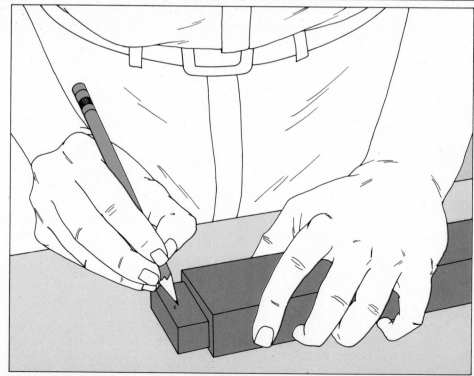

## Two Joints Based on Machine-made Dadoes

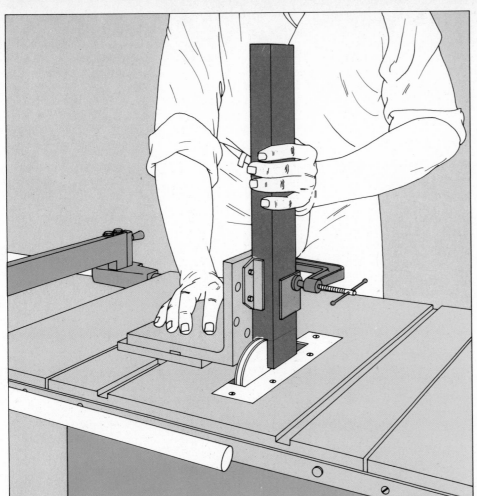

**Slicing a slip joint.** For the mortise of this joint, which is simply a slot cut in the end of a board, mark the end of the board for mortise depth and width. Fit the saw with a dado head of the same width as the mortise, and set the blade height to the mortise depth by holding the mortise board against it. Test the setting on a piece of scrap wood and make necessary adjustments; then, with the mortise board clamped to a tenoning jig (a jig that holds the tenon board upright on one end), make the cut in a single pass. Cut the tenon piece as shown on page 69. If desired, pin the joint for added strength, as shown opposite.

When using this method, keep in mind that mortise depth is limited by the diameter of the dado head. An 8-inch head, for example, can cut no higher than 1¾ inches.

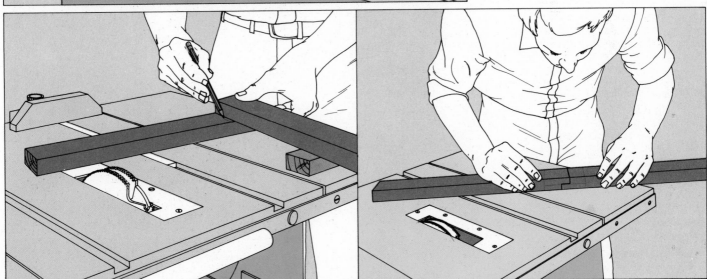

**Spliced ends for lap joints.** Lap the ends of the pieces to be joined over each other at a right angle, and mark shoulder lines on the adjoining faces *(above, left)*. Use a try square to continue the lines around each board, then add a line along the middle of each edge to extend from the shoulder line to the end.

Raise the dado head so that its height is equal to the width of the shoulder— half the thickness of the piece of wood—and then lower it by a half turn of the blade-height crank. Make a test cut at the end of each piece, removing approximately ½ inch of wood, and then fit the two ends together *(above, right)*; make note of how much

deeper the cut needs to be in order to make the pieces flush with each other. Raise the dado head by small degrees, continuing to make test cuts and to test the fit after each pair of cuts. When the two pieces fit together perfectly, cut away the rest of the wood, back as far as the shoulder lines, as on page 69, Step 3.

# Using Dowels to Lock Joints

A blind dowel joint is a kind of lazy man's mortise-and-tenon joint. Hidden wooden pins, projecting finger-like into the two parts, connect them without requiring that the parts be shaped. Most woodworkers can make a blind dowel joint faster than they can cut a mortise and tenon. Unfortunately, the joint does not bear up under great stress as well as a mortise and tenon. Still, dowel joints are sturdy enough to be used in many tables, chairs and cabinet frames.

To make a proper joint, the diameter of the dowel should be one third to one half the thickness of the wood it enters, and it should be ⅛ inch shorter than the combined depth of the two holes into which it fits. In addition, a blind dowel joint should consist of at least two dowels: Paired dowels have much the same ability to resist twisting as does a tenon in a mortise.

The holes must be exactly perpendicular to the board edges into which they are drilled, and matching holes must be perfectly aligned. Such precision is best achieved on a drill press, but not all drill-press tables can be tilted to the true vertical position needed for boring into the ends of boards. Doweling jigs, used in conjunction with a portable drill, offer a suitable alternative. The function of such jigs, which differ in design depending on the manufacturer, is to center a bit guide over the edge of a board and hold the guide at a true right angle. The bit of a portable drill is then inserted in the guide to bore the hole.

Another hole-alignment method uses dowel centers, metal cylinders with raised points in their centers. After a pair of holes has been drilled in one board, a dowel center is inserted, point out, into each hole. The joining piece is then pressed in place against them, and the points mark where the matching holes are to be drilled.

After the holes are made, glue is spread on the ends of the dowels and the sides of the holes; then the dowels are inserted. The dowels, which should be the same diameter as the holes, fit so snugly that they tend to trap air and excess glue in the bottom of the hole. If this happens, the dowels will not penetrate the proper distance. Pressure applied during clamping may force the dowels down, but in the process it may also crack one of the joint pieces.

To prevent air and glue from interfering with the placement of the dowels, escape routes should be provided. You can buy precut dowels, with straight or spiraling grooves, at hardware or lumber stores; or you can cut grooves yourself, using a rasp or a fine-toothed saw. If you are in a hurry, you can even provide an escape route for glue and air by pulling the serrated jaws of pliers down the length of the dowel, impressing it with furrows. Finally, to ease the entry of dowels, you can chamfer their ends with a rasp or sandpaper.

## Drilling Holes for a Blind Dowel Joint

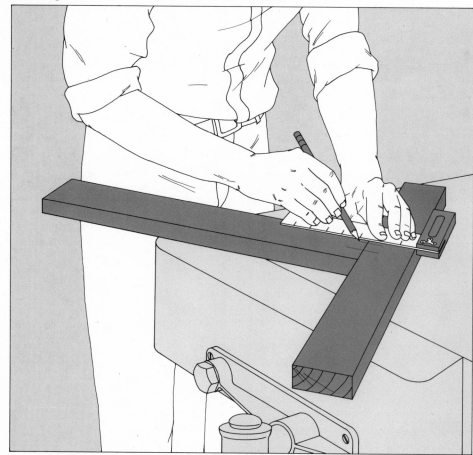

**1** **Marking the dowel locations.** Take the two pieces to be joined and place them face up on a worktable, aligned in their finished position. Then, using a try square, mark a line for each dowel across both boards.

**2** **Boring the holes.** Fit a bit guide of the proper size to a doweling jig, and clamp the jig to one board edge, aligning the jig center line with one of the pencil lines made in Step 1 (*below, left*). Then align the center of the bit guide with the exact center of the board edge. (In the jig shown here, this is achieved by using numerical scales and a thumbscrew to make the adjustment.) Fit the drill with the proper size bit, and add a depth gauge to stop the bit when it has reached the proper depth. Then drill the hole (*below, right*). Reposition the doweling jig to drill additional holes in the board edge. Then drill matching holes in the edge of the adjoining board.

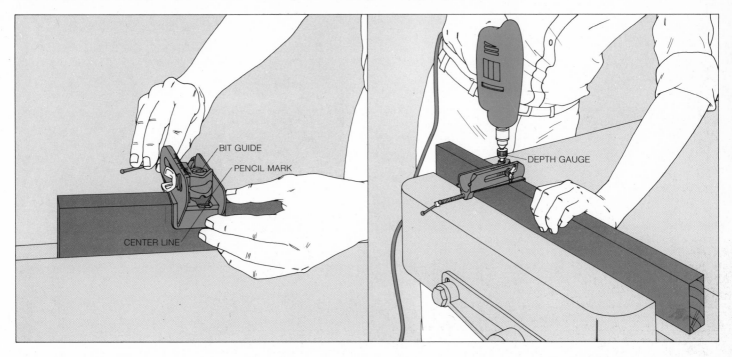

## Preparing and Installing the Dowels

**Grooving the dowels.** Rout a ¼-inch V groove in a length of scrap wood, and lay a dowel in the groove. Clamp both to a worktable and then, with the edge of a rasp or with a fine-toothed saw such as a dovetail saw or a backsaw, cut at least two grooves in the dowel, one down each side. Trim the dowels to size, chamfer the ends, and then spread glue in the holes and on the dowel ends. Insert the dowels into one of the pieces (*inset*), join the pieces, clamp the joint and wipe away excess glue.

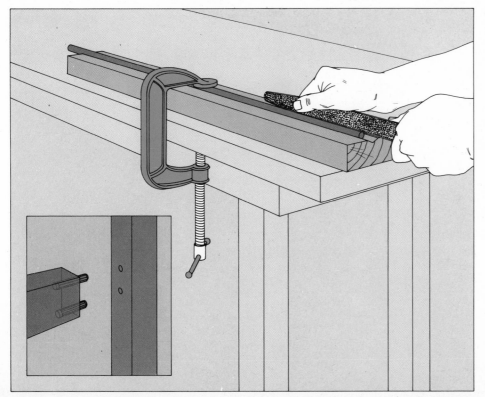

# Miter Joints Reinforced from Inside

A miter joint, precisely cut, will give any corner a clean, finished appearance. In fact, it is the neatness and not the strength of this angled joint that keeps the miter a favorite in the woodworker's repertoire, for the miter is weak compared with other corner bonds. However, if strengthened with plywood splines *(below),* most miter joints have more than enough muscle to hold their own against everyday use and abuse.

Common miter joints are made by cutting 45° angles on two pieces of wood and joining the pieces to form a right-angled corner. There are two categories:

flat joints and edge joints. Flat miters, cut across the face of the wood, are used mostly for decoration—to join the vertical and horizontal strips that cover the front edges of many cabinets, for example, especially those built of plywood. Picture frames, too, are almost always made with flat miter joints. Edge miters are made by cutting a bevel along each of the two edges to be joined and are used in case construction—to join the four sides of a basic box-shaped cabinet.

Splines, thin slivers of wood that slip into grooves cut along the adjoining faces of both flat and edge miter joints,

are commonly made from ⅛-inch plywood. If you use plywood of this thickness, the spline grooves can be quickly and accurately cut with the regular ⅛-inch blade of a table saw. For a stronger joint in thicker wood, use a ¼-inch dado blade to cut the grooves and ¼-inch plywood to make the spline. Test-fit a spline joint before gluing it together.

Although almost any hand or power saw can be used to cut the miters, the table saw is the tool most woodworkers prefer. It makes angled cuts easily and precisely, especially when used with the simple jig described on page 76.

**Three miter joints and splines.** The three miter joints shown here, all reinforced with plywood splines, are appropriate—each in its own way—in many different woodworking situations. The diagonal-spline miter is used for edge joints; the spline, set diagonal to the faces of the wood, runs the entire length of the joint. A triangular-spline miter is used for the flat miter joints found in frame construction; such a spline is set into the outside corner of the joint. A blind-spline miter, used either in edge construction, as shown, or in frame construction, has a spline that is invisible on the outer edge of the joint; it combines strength with neat appearance.

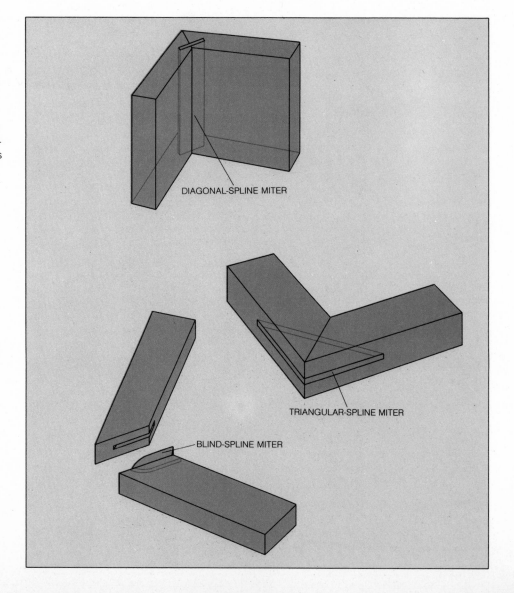

DIAGONAL-SPLINE MITER

TRIANGULAR-SPLINE MITER

BLIND-SPLINE MITER

## Setting a Diagonal Spline into a Mitered Edge

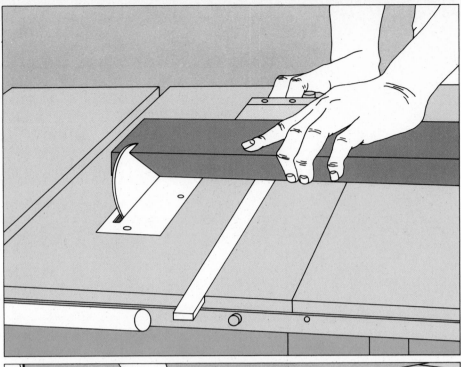

**1** **Making the bevel cuts.** To bevel the ends of the boards, remove the blade guard from a table saw and set the blade at a 45° angle; set the miter gauge at a 90° angle. Turn on the saw. With one hand holding the board flat against the table and firmly against the miter gauge, push the miter gauge forward with the other hand, directing the end of the board through the blade. Then cut the second board; the top faces of the two boards will be on the outside of the joint.

To set up the saw for cutting the spline groove, lower the blade to a height of ⅜ inch, but leave it tilted at a 45° angle. Remove the miter gauge from its channel, and install the rip fence so that the blade tilts away from it. Lay one cut board on the table, beveled end against the fence and bevel facing down, and bring the fence toward the blade until the lower edge of the bevel is lined up with the edge of the saw slot; lock the fence in this position.

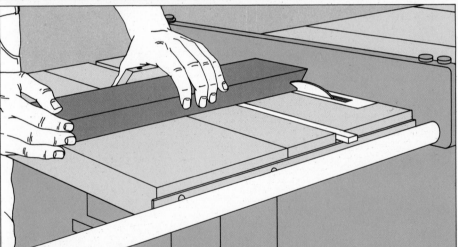

**2** **Cutting grooves for the spline.** Hold the board firmly against the table with one hand and against the rip fence with the other while you push the board past the blade, cutting a groove into the beveled surface ¹⁄₁₆ inch above its lower edge. Cut the second board in the same way. Return the blade to a vertical position and attach the blade guard. Then move the rip fence to the other side of the blade.

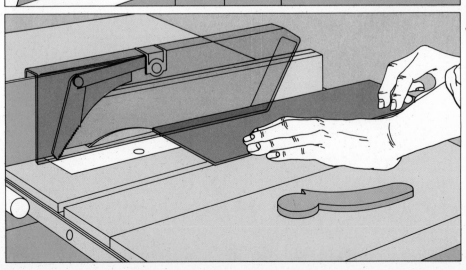

**3** **Cutting the spline.** With the blade guard in place, cut the spline from ⅛-inch plywood. First butt a piece of plywood against the fence, and push it past the blade to obtain a strip ¾ inch wide; use a push stick to protect your fingers as you approach the end of the cut. Then, using a miter gauge instead of the fence, cut off a section of the plywood strip the same length as the beveled edges of the joint.

**4** **Assembling the joint.** Place the two boards on edge, bevel to bevel, on a flat surface. Coat both beveled ends and both faces of the spline with yellow glue. Slip one spline edge into a groove, and then push the groove of the second board over the other edge of the spline. Press firmly, check the joint for alignment, then wipe away any excess glue and clamp the joint *(page 82)* until the glue has dried.

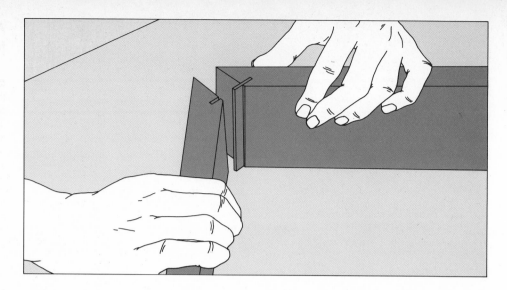

## An Angled Jig for Cutting Flat Miter Joints

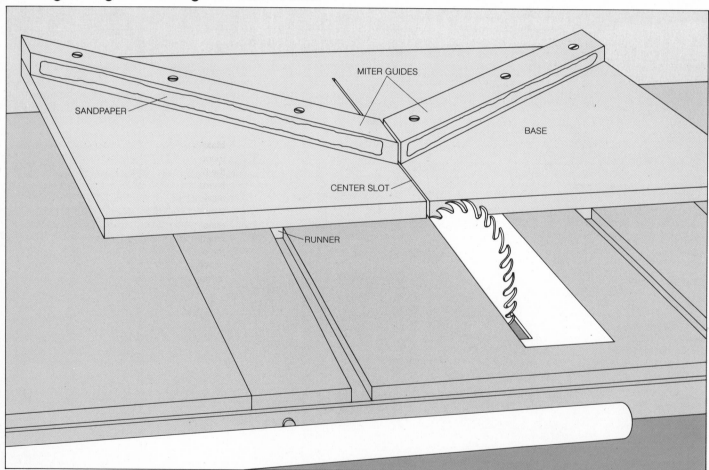

SANDPAPER

MITER GUIDES

BASE

CENTER SLOT

RUNNER

**Cutting multiple miters.** A miter jig lets you cut a series of identical miter joints on the table saw with a minimum of adjusting. Boards already cut to length are held against the inner faces of the two angled miter guides as the jig is pushed past the blade; longer boards are held against the outer faces of the guides.

The base of the jig, which slides across the table on runners that fit in the miter-gauge channels, is a 20-by-30-inch rectangle of ½-inch plywood. A ⅛-inch center slot, cut two thirds of the way across the base, provides passage for the blade as the jig is pushed across the table. The miter guides, made of 1-by-2-inch hard-

wood, are screwed to the base to form a right angle and trimmed even at the far edges. The inner ends are mitered at 45° angles and meet at the center slot, about 6 inches from the edge of the base. A strip of sandpaper is glued to the inner and outer faces of each guide to keep the boards from slipping as they are cut.

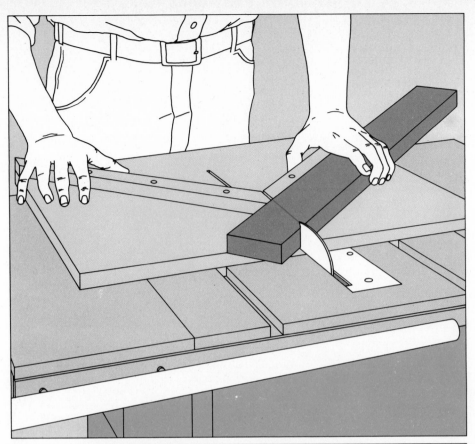

## A Triangular Spline for a Mitered Corner

**1** **Cutting and assembling the miter joint.** Mark the location of the miters on the edges of the boards to be joined, and position the mitering jig (*opposite, bottom*) on the saw table. Then set a board on the jig, against a miter guide, lining up the mark on the board with the center slot. Turn on the saw and, holding the board firmly against the miter guide, push the jig across the blade until the board is cut. Return the jig to its starting position, and cut the second board in the same way, holding it against the opposite miter guide. Apply glue to the joint and clamp it, using a corner clamp (*page 80*).

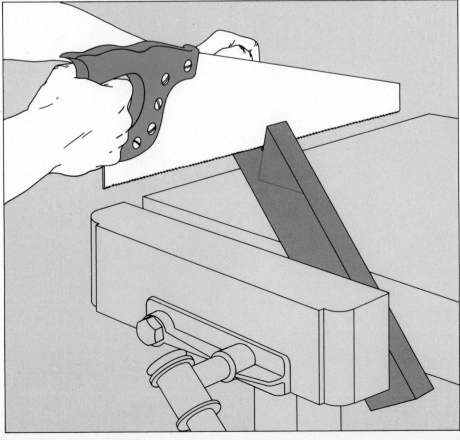

**2** **Making a jig for the triangular groove.** Cut a triangular notch in one edge of a 2-by-4, making the base of the triangle at the edge of the board 5½ inches long. To outline the notch, first mark off a 5½-inch length on one edge of the 2-by-4; then use a T bevel to draw lines from the ends of the base on the face of the board, meeting to form a right angle ¾ inch short of the opposite edge. Cut out the triangle with a handsaw. Then trim away the ends of the 2-by-4, leaving a jig 8 inches long.

**3** **Cutting a triangular groove.** Set the corner of the glued miter joint in the triangular jig, and position the jig on the saw table so that the center of the joint is aligned with the blade. Then adjust a tenoning jig *(page 71)* to hold the assembly in place *(below, left)*, and clamp one leg of the miter joint to the tenoning jig.

Raise the blade until the height is just short of the center of the miter joint; then turn on the saw and, holding the joint-and-jig assembly steady with one hand, push the tenoning jig forward with the other hand until the blade has cut through the triangular jig and all the way across the corner of the miter joint *(below, right)*.

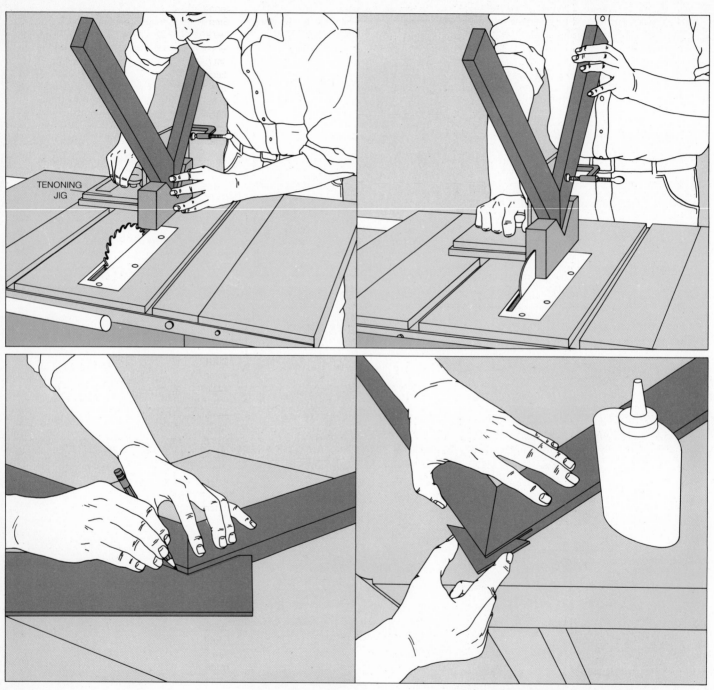

TENONING
JIG

**4** **Tracing and cutting a triangular spline.** Slide a piece of ⅛-inch plywood into the triangular groove you have cut, and outline the right angle formed by the outside edge of the joint *(above, left)*. Cut out the spline, spread glue on both sides and fit it into the groove *(above, right)*. Clamp the faces of the joint until the glue dries, then sand off protruding spline edges.

## Cutting a Hidden Slot for a Blind Spline

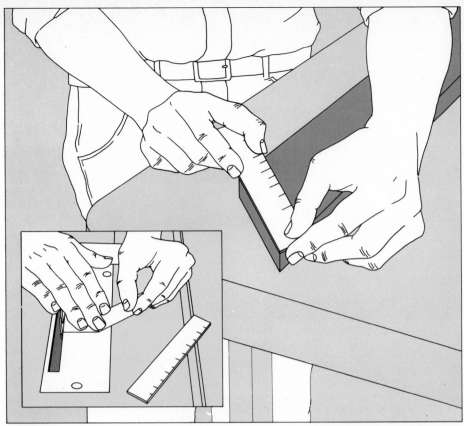

**1** **Measuring for the spline groove.** After mitering the ends of the adjoining boards (*page 77, Step 1*), measure the length of the miter. With two strips of masking tape, mark off three quarters of this length on the left side of the blade slot (*inset*). Place the first strip of tape perpendicular to the slot, aligning one edge of the tape with the point where the saw teeth protrude from the slot; then measure along the slot a distance equal to three quarters of the miter length, and mark the point with a second strip of tape, also perpendicular to the slot.

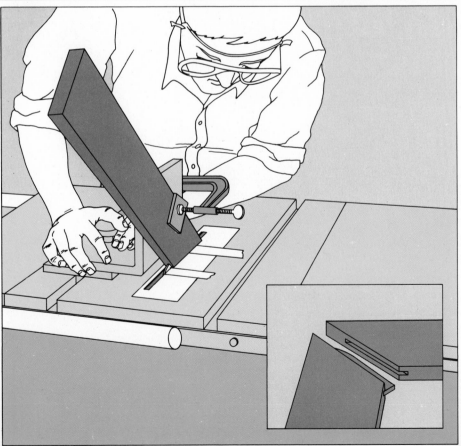

**2** **Cutting grooves for the spline.** Clamp one mitered board to a tenoning jig, mitered end flat against the table, board slanting away from you. Adjust the height of the blade and the jig assembly to cut a groove ⅜ inch deep into the center of the mitered end. Then turn on the saw, and push the jig forward until the far edge of the board meets the edge of the masking tape that marks three quarters of the length of the miter. Stop the saw and pull the board back, away from the blade. Cut a matching groove in the mitered end of the second board in the same way.

Cut a rectangular spline from a ¾-inch-wide strip of ⅛-inch plywood, as long as the exposed edge of the grooves. Use a coping saw to trim one end of the spline into a tongue shape, matching the curve of the grooves. Test-fit the shape of the spline by assembling the joint without glue (*inset*); when the spline fits, spread glue on the spline and the mitered ends, and clamp the joint together. After the glue is dry, use a coping saw to trim the end of the spline that protrudes from the inside corner of the joint.

# Clamping Work of Varied Shapes and Sizes

Good glue joints require pressure during the final phase of assembly, for without it the glue will not penetrate the wood. But applying pressure is often more than a matter of turning a screw. The pressure must conform to the anatomy of the joint and to the contours of the surfaces being joined. You must choose the right clamp for the job or, lacking the proper clamp, you must improvise one. For some joints, especially those involving irregular surfaces, you may have to fashion clamp accouterments from wood scraps.

The devices and techniques shown on the following pages solve the most common clamping problems. Some of the devices eliminate the need for clamps or reduce the number needed for the job. Some of the techniques call for specially shaped cauls—pieces of wood that fit between the clamps and the work being joined—to adapt odd shapes to the flat surfaces of standard clamp jaws.

The same basic principles apply to all these methods of clamping, whether straightforward or inventive. First, the joint should be assembled without glue and tested for fit in the clamping appara-

tus. Then, after the glue is applied and the joint is reassembled, pressure from the clamping should be applied evenly so that the pieces are not shifted out of alignment or out of square.

When the clamping involves several points of pressure, it usually is best to tighten center clamps first, then work toward the ends, checking the alignment with a try square or a T bevel. And the pressure should be firm but not severe: Excess force will squeeze so much glue into the wood pores that not enough will remain on the surfaces to act as a bond.

## Choosing the Right Clamp for the Job

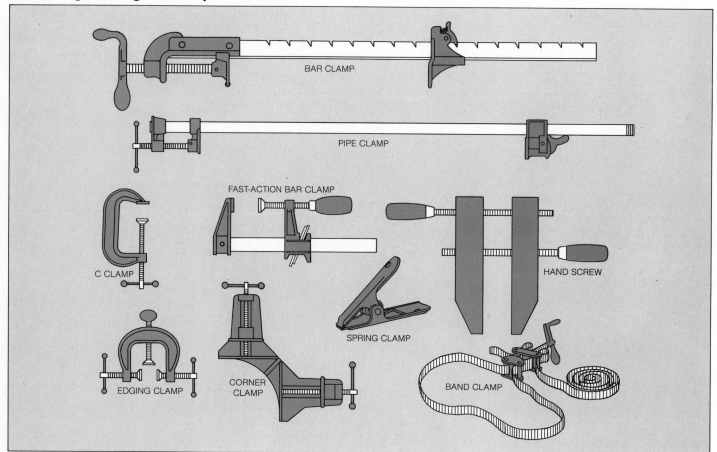

BAR CLAMP

PIPE CLAMP

FAST-ACTION BAR CLAMP

C CLAMP

HAND SCREW

SPRING CLAMP

EDGING CLAMP

CORNER CLAMP

BAND CLAMP

**A catalogue of clamps.** Quick and easy to use, the clothespin-like spring clamp is the best choice for thin, delicate pieces of wood. Where greater pressure is required, C clamps suffice if the joint pieces can fit within the jaws; some open to 12 inches. The wooden jaws of a hand screw open as much as 17 inches and can be adjusted to fit nonparallel surfaces. The fast-action bar clamp spans even wider distances; a spring-

activated lever locks and unlocks the clamp in one quick motion.

Although a bar clamp is the best choice for large assemblies because of its strength, its close cousin, the pipe clamp, has advantages of adaptability and economy: The two fittings slip over ordinary steel plumbing pipe of any length. A band clamp, with its long flexible tape, can hug the

joints of large irregular structures, such as chairs. The E-shaped edging clamp and the arced corner clamp are designed to fit specific joints. The threaded spindles on the arms of an edging clamp will grip two faces of a board; the middle spindle presses molding against the board edge. The jaws of a corner clamp fit against perpendicular boards and apply pressure from two directions to clamp a right-angled joint.

# Homemade Substitutes for Store-bought Clamps

**An edging caul.** The slightly concave edge of this long, narrow caul, clamped near the middle of two joined pieces—here a shelf and its edge molding—evenly distributes the pressure of just two clamps out to the ends of the pieces. The caul works equally well on pieces shorter than its own length.

To make an edging caul, scribe a gentle arc on a 2-inch-wide length of oak, maple or birch, making the arc ¼ inch higher at its midpoint than at its ends; the wood for the caul should be as thick as the width of the piece it will press. Cut the curve on a band saw, or use hand shaping tools *(page 97)*, and sand it smooth. Then place the concave edge *(inset)* against the work being glued, and apply the clamps. For cauls shorter than 2 feet, only one clamp is necessary.

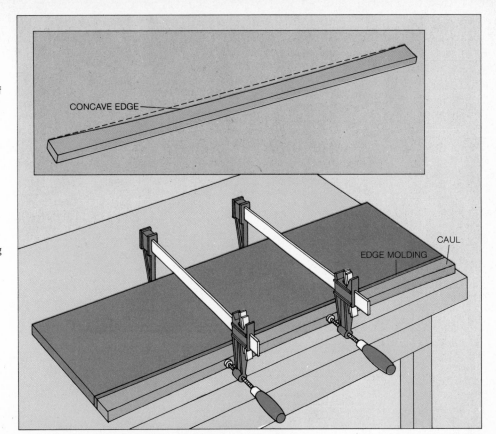

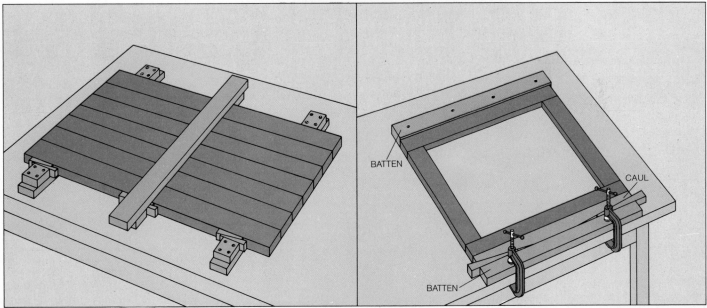

**Homemade bar clamps.** If you do not own bar clamps, you can duplicate their effect with two techniques, both of which use hardwood strips and wedges. In one method, you fabricate imitation bar clamps *(above, left)*; in the other, you force the far side of a joint against a wooden stop *(above, right)*.

For the first method, shown here clamping board edges, begin by screwing square blocks to the ends of hardwood battens. Then place alternate battens on opposite faces of the joined boards, and gently drive wedges between the blocks and the board edges. For the second method, first screw or clamp a batten to the worktable. Butt the far side of the joined pieces, here forming a cabinetry frame, against it. To the near side, add a hardwood caul, trimmed at the ends so that it will accommodate wedges. Butt a second batten against the trimmed edge of the

caul, and clamp the second batten firmly to the worktable. Then drive wedges as needed between the second batten and the caul.

When you are using either one of these substitute bar clamps, it is necessary to cut the wedges long and thin. A 4-inch wedge should not be any more than ¾ inch wide at its large end and ¼ inch at its small end. Make the wedges of hardwood if you are intending to use them often.

# One-of-a-kind Cauls for Unique Situations

**Cauls for curves.** Held by two C clamps, these two semicircular cauls distribute pressure around new tabletop edging. The cauls are made of ¼-inch lath, with 1-by-1 blocks glued to the ends.

Equally useful on any continuous curve, this type of caul is always made specifically to fit the individual project. Each lath piece is cut ¼ inch shorter than half the circumference of the piece being clamped, leaving a ¼-inch gap between blocks before clamping. The block length may vary from ¾ inch to 2 inches, depending on the curve: for a shallow curve, use a long block; for a tight curve, a short block.

**A contoured caul for rounded edging.** Curved on one side to conform to the half-round edging that is being glued to a tabletop, this shaped caul provides a flat surface on the other side for the jaw of a pipe clamp. A lip on the caul hooks under the bottom of the edging, to hold it vertically as well as horizontally when the pipe clamp is tightened (*inset*).

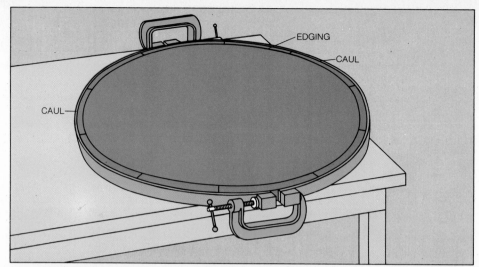

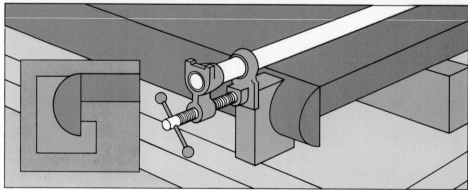

# Devices That Hold Miter Joints Together

**Adding blocks.** Pairs of triangular blocks glued to the sides of a mitered corner create parallel clamping surfaces. Brown paper glued between the blocks and the mitered pieces makes it easier, once the joint is set, to knock off the blocks with a hammer and to sand away residue.

To begin this clamping technique, cut right triangles from ¾-inch boards; glue brown paper to the side that has the lengthwise grain. Notch the side diagonal to the grain, to accommodate the jaws of a C clamp. Then glue the blocks, in pairs, to the mitered pieces, paper-covered side facing in; clamp the blocks until the glue sets (*inset, top*). Then remove the clamps, spread glue on the mitered cuts and assemble the joint, reattaching the clamps to the blocks.

If the joint to be assembled is not a right angle, shape the blocks to fit the angle. The angle between the paper-covered side of the block and the side that holds the clamp (angle A) should be equal to angle B—one half the angle of the miter joint (*inset, bottom*).

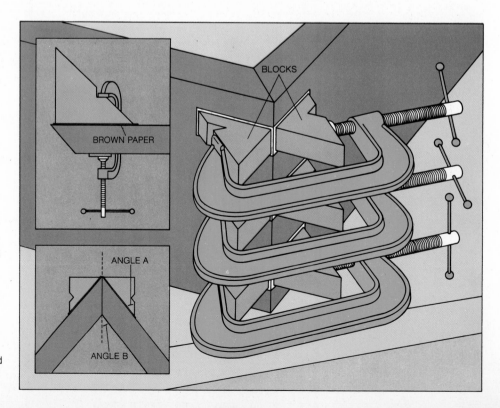

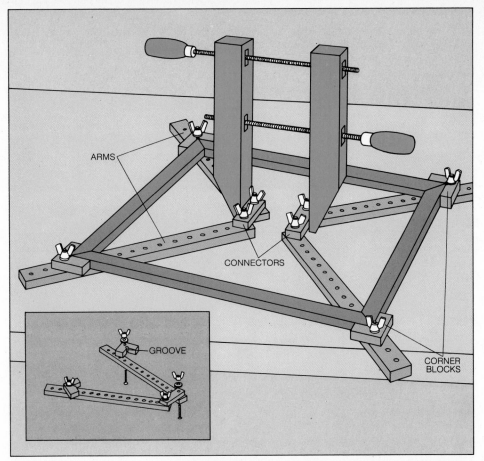

**A wooden jig for mitered frames.** Clamped by one hand screw, the two identical halves of this adjustable jig pull together the four mitered corners of a frame. The corner blocks can be positioned at 1-inch intervals along the length of the arms to grip frames of varying size.

To make the jig, cut four hardwood arms that are ¾ inch thick, 2 inches wide and as long as needed for the frames you intend to glue. Drill holes down their center lines every inch for $5/16$-inch bolts. Join each pair of arms with hardwood connectors, cut to span the last two holes and held in place with bolts, washers and wing nuts (*inset*). Cut the four angled corner blocks from hardwood also, and hollow out a shallow groove along their inside corners to provide an escape route for excess glue squeezed from the miter joint. Drill holes in the blocks to match the holes in the arms, and secure them to the arms with wing nuts, bolts and washers.

ARMS

CONNECTORS

GROOVE

CORNER BLOCKS

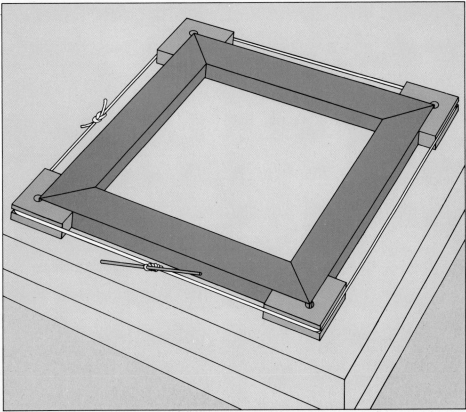

**Applying pressure with a tourniquet.** A strong cord encircling four corner blocks and twisted by a dowel makes a simple clamp that can solve difficult problems. The blocks that clasp the pieces being joined have horizontal grooves for the cord and shallow vertical grooves along their inside corners to serve as escape routes for excess glue. To tighten the clamp, twist the cord with the dowel, then fix the dowel in place by bracing it between the work and the tabletop. The blocks can be cut to fit any shape—pentagons, hexagons, even asymmetrical joinings that defy the grip of conventional clamps.

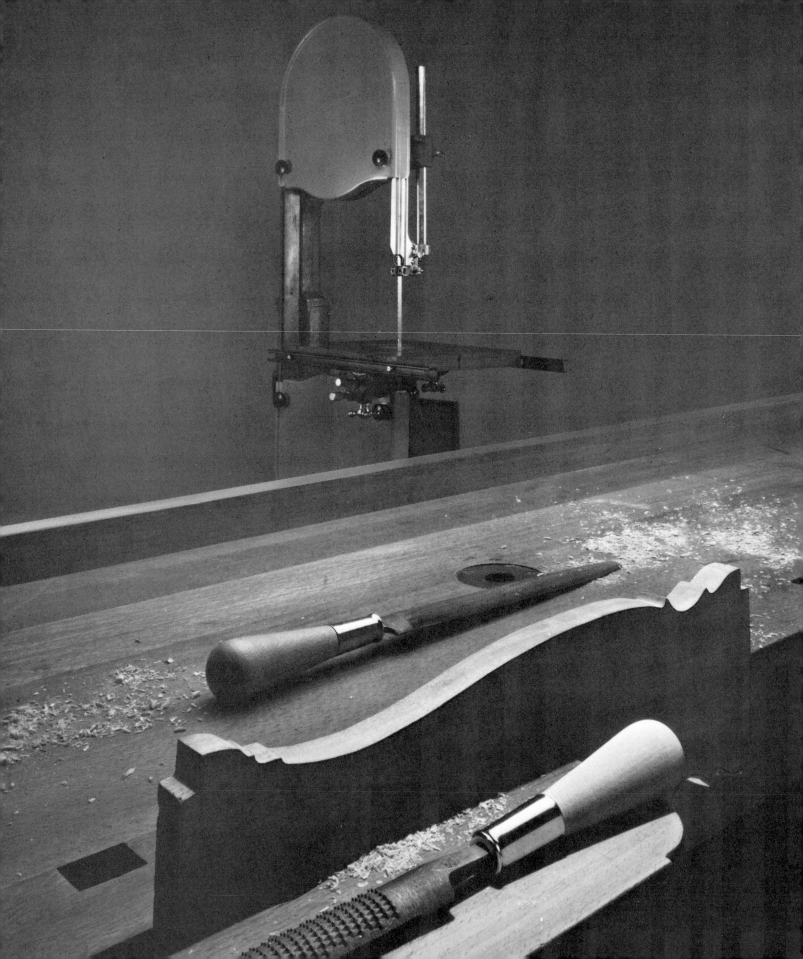

# 3 Shaping by Hand or Machine

**Taking the curves in high.** A rasp and file smooth and refine the reverse curves of a chair back whose mandolin shape was roughed out with the band saw in the background. The band saw speeds a task that once had to be done with hand saws. But the rasp and the file, with their myriad tiny teeth, continue to be the preferred tools for finishing intricate shapes—just as they have been for centuries.

In years past, the shaping of wood was done primarily with hand tools, and the pitfalls of inexperience were overcome during long years of apprenticeship. Under the tutelage of a master craftsman, the aspiring woodworker learned about wood by holding it in his hands, sensing in his fingers its resistance or pliancy under every stroke of the drawknife and every probe of the gouge. He learned that when a spokeshave began to buck or chatter in the middle of a cut, it was fighting against the grain—that it was time to shift his tool and cut in the opposite direction. And he knew that if he tried to carve soft wood into a spindle, his chisel would pull on the soft grain and produce a ragged, uneven contour.

Today power tools do in minutes the tedious shaping jobs that once took hours of work—a boon to home craftsmen, for whom woodworking is likely to be a part-time hobby. A band saw, for instance, can be used to trim away surrounding waste wood, quickly defining an intricate shape even in very thick stock. Used with care—and a little imagination—the saw's continuous blade will make fast work of difficult jobs such as roughing out a cabriole leg or rounding a broad tabletop. Equally effective are the power sanding tools that can grind out complex shapes, either gentle or severe.

But the speed and almost instantaneous facility that power tools provide can be a mixed blessing to the novice. To a degree, power tools may preclude knowledge that can be acquired only through the intimacy of touch. Indeed, some expert woodcraft instructors discourage any use of power tools until the woodworker has mastered hand tools. This approach is rigorous but not without merit. The principal advantage of working with a hand tool is that each stroke of the tool can be adapted to the specific piece of wood. If a surface is knotted, tool pressure is lessened to avoid tearing out the knot. If the wood grain swirls, its pattern can be followed for the smoothest possible cut. Thus, working with hand tools forces the woodworker to learn as much about the material as about the tools.

The truth is that both hand and power tools have a place in shaping wood. Past craftsmen learned how to minimize their efforts—they knew when to switch from a heavy tool, such as a drawknife, to a delicate one, such as a thumb plane. Modern woodworkers develop the same instincts. They learn to let their power tools bear the brunt of the work, then finish the job with hand tools. If a band saw, jig saw or power sander will speed up a job, they are put to use. But when the shortcuts are over and the final contours are to be cut, only hand-tool precision will do. At this point, wood shaping is the same demanding craft it has always been. It requires patience, methodical care and a certain reverence for wood.

# Cutting Curves in Wood with Power Tools

Curved wood that ultimately appears in graceful furniture and architectural trim begins to take shape, nine times out of ten, on a band saw. This large power tool *(page 17)* saves the modern woodworker hours of time in cutting rough curves, which can later be refined with hand tools *(page 94)*. You can cut almost any curved design on a band saw if you know the tricks that enable you to cope with the saw's limitations.

Because the saw blade is a continuous steel band that moves in an elongated oval, the most rigid of the tool's limitations is the distance between the cutting edge of the blade and the housing for the return side of the blade. In home-shop models, this throat is only 10 ot 14 inches wide, so the width of wood that can pass through is very limited.

To keep the throat width from blocking your progress when you cut large shapes, you may have to stop in the middle of a cut and saw through a waste area to the edge of the board, then begin the cut again in another direction. You can also turn off the saw and backtrack cut through the cut already made, in order to change direction. If nothing else works,

you can draw guidelines on both sides of the wood so that you can turn the board over when necessary. In some cases, as in cutting the circular tabletop on pages 89-91, you can make a jig that allows you to cut a large shape in spite of the restrictions imposed by the throat width.

Smaller curves present fewer difficulties unless they are so small that the blade cannot follow them without binding. Strategically placed pilot holes and tangential or radial cuts through waste wood *(pages 88-89)* provide the solutions to many of these problems.

Using the right blade for the job will also help you overcome the tool's limitations. The most commonly used blade is ¼ inch wide; it will cut a curve with a radius as small as ⅝ inch in wood up to 1½ inches thick. There are narrower blades for ever tighter curves—a ⅛-inch blade will cut a curve with a ¼-inch radius, but only in wood no thicker than ¾ inch. Wider blades will cut thicker wood, but as the width increases the possibility of cutting tight curves decreases. Blades ¾ inch and wider will cut shallow curves in lumber up to 6 inches thick.

When curves are too tight and the

work too fine to be managed on a band saw, the smaller, less powerful jig saw is the alternative. It can be fitted with a variety of delicate blades, some of them as narrow as .03 inch.

The blade on a jig saw moves up and down rapidly rather than spinning in a continuous band and, since both ends of the blade can be detached, the saw can cut out curved sections inside a pattern, where no waste area leads to the cut. A pilot hole drilled through the pattern provides the starting point; the blade is inserted through the hole *(page 93)*.

Cutting curves on a band saw or a jig saw requires extra care: Note the special safety rules on page 9. A push stick is impractical for guiding wood through a curved cut, so your hands will be close to the blade as you guide the wood. Try to keep your fingers at least 3 inches from the blade at all times.

Never force the wood forward when you cut curves—the blade may snap.

Before making any cut, be sure all parts of the tool are properly adjusted. For setting blade guides and adjusting blade tension on a band saw, see page 18. Jig-saw instructions are on page 93.

## Guiding a Band Saw along a Simple Curve

**Cutting a curve.** Lay out the curve on the stock, place the wood on the saw table, adjust the blade guide and turn on the saw. Push the board forward with one hand, guiding it with the other so that the cut is slightly on the waste side of the guideline. Apply steady, constant pressure, pushing as fast as the blade will easily cut. The correct amount of pressure is important: If you push too slowly or stop in the middle of a cut, the spinning blade will burn the wood; if you push too hard, you may break the blade or make an uneven cut.

For a long cut, or if your progress is blocked by the saw's throat, take the blade out of the wood through the waste area; then reposition the board, and cut back in from another point.

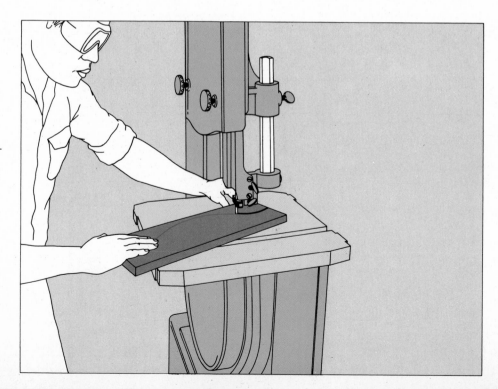

**Cutting parallel curves.** To draw a curve parallel to one already cut, set the legs of a carpenter's compass to the planned width of the finished piece, then move the compass point along the cut curve so that the pencil point scribes a corresponding second guideline on the wood. Be sure that you are holding the compass perpendicular to the two points of contact. Set the blade guide and cut the second curve.

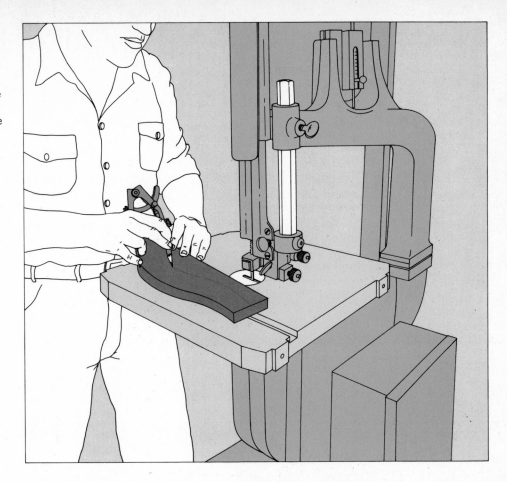

## Cutting Stacked Boards for Identical Curves

**Cutting several pieces at once.** Cut a stack of thin boards in one operation to obtain a set of identical curved shapes. Draw the pattern on one piece of wood or plywood, then stack similar pieces under the pattern piece to form a pile no higher than 6 inches. Drive finishing nails through the waste corners of the stack so that the points protrude through the piece on which you have drawn the pattern. Then put the stack of pieces on the saw table, turn on the saw and cut along the guideline.

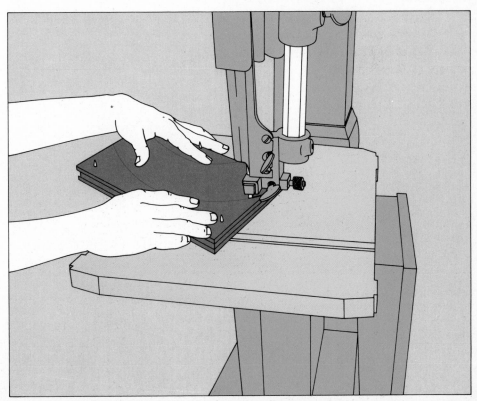

# Adapting the Saw to Scrolls and Circles

**A turning hole for a tight inside curve.** Use a hand drill or a drill press *(page 67)* to cut turning holes that will give you room to maneuver the saw blade inside a tight curve. Drill each hole so that a section of its circumference touches the curved guideline. To cut around the curve, follow the guideline until you reach the hole, then take the blade through the hole without stopping the saw and continue following the guideline on the other side.

To make a square inside corner, first drill a round pilot hole in the corner, then use a chisel and a mallet *(page 67)* to square off the corner *(inset)*. Run the saw blade along the guideline into the hole; then turn the wood 90° and continue cutting along the guideline.

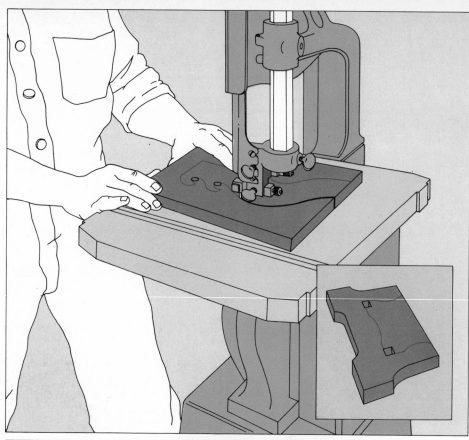

**Tangential cuts for a sharp outside curve.** Use tangential cuts to maneuver around the outside of a sharp curve if the saw blade binds. Start the cut on as straight a section of the guideline as possible, and cut toward the curve. When the blade begins to bind, veer off the guideline and off the edge of the board, cutting away a section of the waste area *(inset)*. Stop the saw, remove the waste section from the saw table, and resume the cut on the guideline, moving the wood along until the blade starts to bind again. Then make another tangential cut. Repeat as necessary to round the curve.

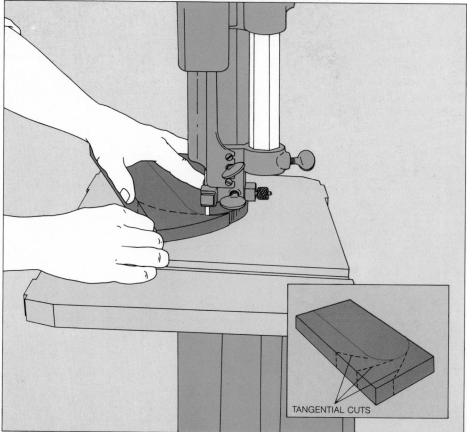

TANGENTIAL CUTS

**Radial cuts for a tight, continuous curve.** To ease the saw blade around the outside of a tight, continuous curve—in this example a small disk—first make a series of radial cuts from the edges of the board through the waste area toward the circle. Space the cuts ½ to 1 inch apart, arranged like the spokes of a wheel. Stop each cut slightly short of the guideline. Later, as you are cutting around the outside of the circle, the pieces of waste wood will fall off.

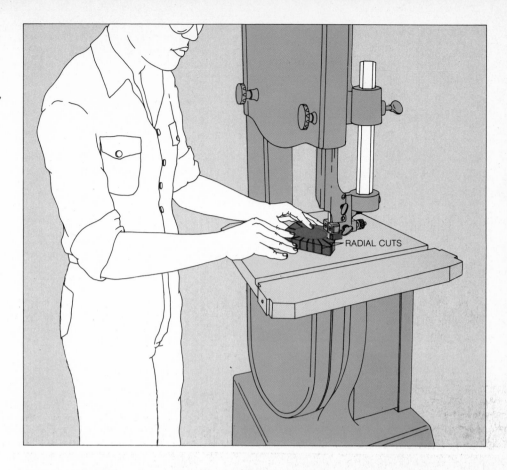

## Setting Up a Jig to Saw a Large Circular Shape

**1** **Enlarging the saw table.** Cut two 2-by-4s to equal the length of the saw table plus the radius of the planned disk. Tilt the throat end of the saw table up, and fasten the 2-by-4s to the table's sides with screws driven through the predrilled holes in the table edges. Be sure that the top edge of each 2-by-4 is flush with the tabletop and that one end of each is flush with the edge of the table nearest the throat.

From ½-inch plywood, cut a rectangle 2 inches wider than the distance between the outside faces of the 2-by-4s and 12 inches longer than the radius of the planned disk.

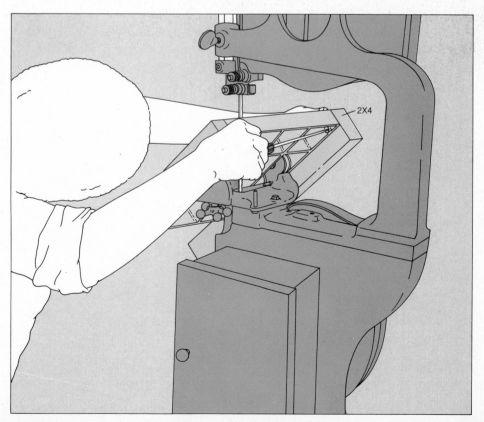

**2** **Cutting the jig.** Place the plywood rectangle *(page 89, Step 1)* on the saw table, so that about 6 inches of it is to the left of the blade. Turn on the saw, and cut until the far edge of the board overhangs the far 2-by-4 by 1 inch; stop the saw but leave the board in place.

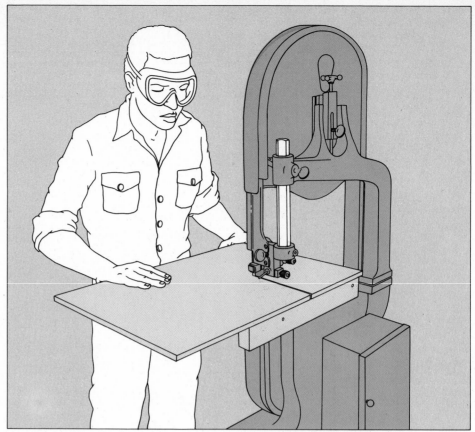

**3** **Marking the radius and installing a pivot.** Place a framing square on top of the plywood, with the short arm toward you, the corner just touching the cutting edge of the blade, and the long arm to the right of and perpendicular to the side of the blade. Measuring on the long arm, draw a line out from the blade, equal in length to the radius of the disk you are going to cut. Mark the end of the line, indicating the center of the disk. Remove the plywood from the table without turning on the saw.

Drill a pilot hole through the plywood at the disk's center point and, from the underside of the board, drive a 2-inch screw through the hole until its tip protrudes ¼ inch *(inset, Step 4)*. The tip will serve as a pivot while the disk is cut.

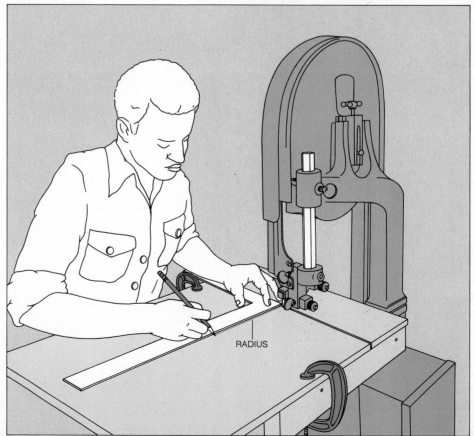

RADIUS

**4** **Fastening the jig to the saw table.** Reposition the plywood on the saw table by sliding the kerf past the stationary blade, and clamp the plywood in place. Then drill two pilot holes through the jig edges into each 2-by-4, countersinking the holes for the screwheads. Fasten the jig to the 2-by-4s with 1½-inch flat-head screws.

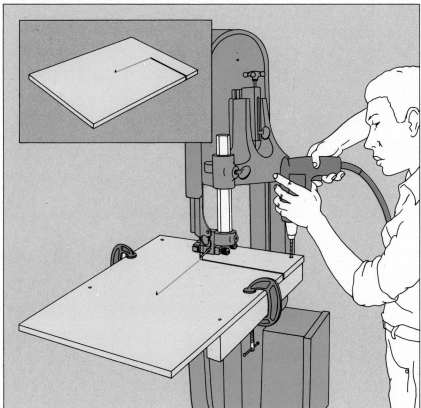

**5** **Marking the stock for cutting.** Square off the stock from which you plan to cut the large disk (*pages 14-16*), then draw a guideline for an entrance cut. To do this, first draw two corner-to-corner diagonal lines on the underside of the stock; the point where they intersect will be the center of the disk. Measuring with a framing square, draw a line the length of the planned radius, extending out from the center point. From the end of this radius line, draw a perpendicular entrance-cut guideline extending to the edge of the stock. Transfer this final line to the top side.

At the center point on the underside, make a dimple ⅛ inch deep by tapping a center punch or a nail set into the wood with a mallet.

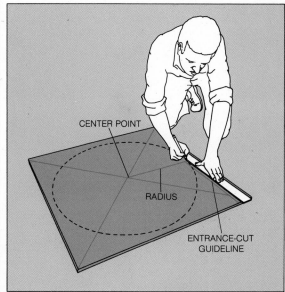

CENTER POINT

RADIUS

ENTRANCE-CUT GUIDELINE

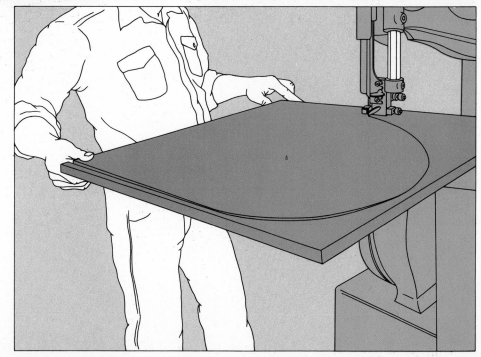

**6** **Cutting the disk.** Retract the pivot screw at the center of the jig so that its tip no longer protrudes. Place the stock right side up on the jig, cut to the end of the entrance-cut guideline, and stop the saw. Reach under the jig, screw the pivot screw back up to protrude ¼ inch and, looking between the jig and the stock, gently maneuver the stock until the dimple at the center rests on the tip of the pivot screw. Turn the saw on again and feed the stock into the blade, rotating the wood on the pivot screw until the disk has been completely cut.

## Outlining the Profile of a Compound Curve

**1** **Drawing the guidelines.** Make a paper template of the curved shape to be rough-cut—in this example, a cabriole chair leg—and square off a piece of wood to encompass the widest dimensions of the shape *(pages 14-16)*. Trace the template on one face of the stock, turn the template over, and trace it on an adjoining face so that identical parts meet at the same points along one edge of the stock *(inset)*.

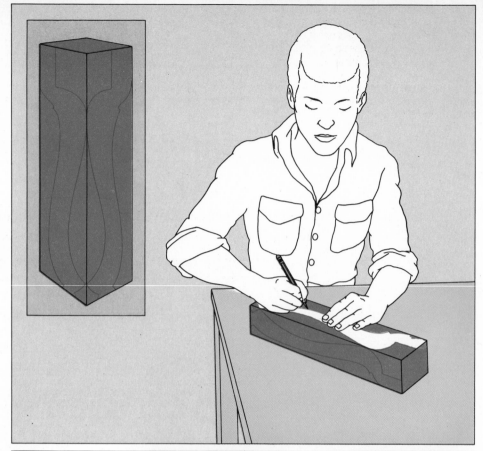

**2** **Making the first pair of cuts.** Set the stock on the saw table with one outlined profile facing up; cut along both sides of the profile. Then tack the waste wood back in place temporarily *(inset)*, taking care not to drive a nail into any area that will be part of the finished shape.

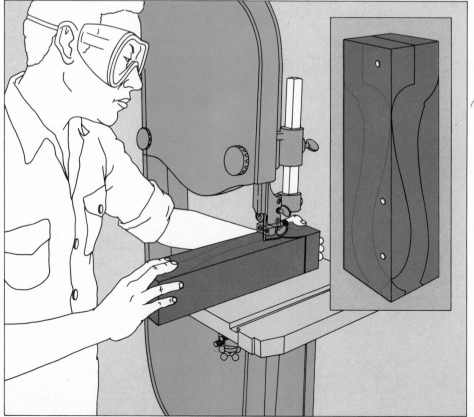

**3** **Making the second pair of cuts.** Set the stock on the saw table so that the second pair of guidelines are facing up; cut the one on the left first, as shown, then the one on the right. Discard all sections of waste wood.

To smooth and finish the roughed-out shape, use the hand tools and the techniques that are described on pages 94-99.

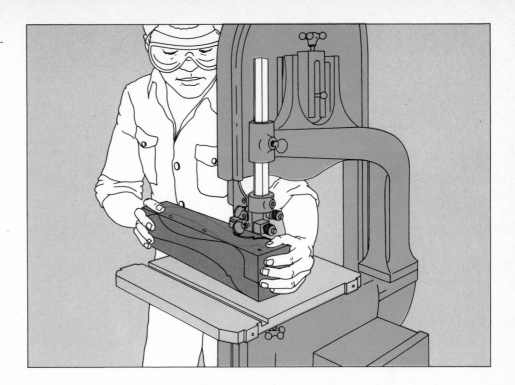

## Making an Inside Cut with a Jig Saw

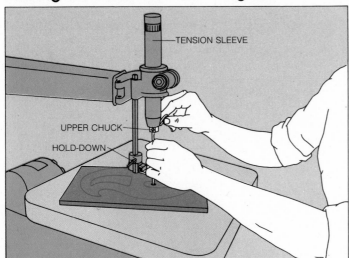

TENSION SLEEVE

UPPER CHUCK

HOLD-DOWN

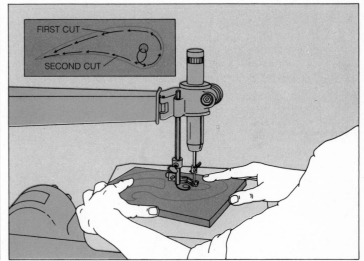

FIRST CUT

SECOND CUT

**1** **Setting the blade for the cut.** Drill a pilot hole through the wood within the guidelines for the curved section to be cut out; then place the wood on the saw table, with the pilot hole directly beneath the empty upper chuck. Slip the saw blade through the pilot hole, the teeth pointing downward, and tighten the upper and lower chucks around the ends of the blade (*inset*). Adjust the spring mechanism so that the hold-down is barely touching the top of the wood.

**2** **Making the cut.** Turn on the saw, and feed the wood into the blade until you reach the guideline. If all the curves in the cutout are gradual, make the cut in one continuous pass, feeding the wood so that the blade follows the guideline all the way around the cutout to the starting position. Turn off the saw and disassemble the saw blade; remove the work from the saw table.

If, as shown, there is a point in the curve where the blade will be unable to turn, follow the guideline around the gradual curves until the blade can go no farther. Stop the saw, and backtrack along the kerf into the pilot hole; then cut along the guideline in a different direction, to the point where you stopped before (*inset*).

# Contouring Wood with Hand Tools

Wood grain, with its flowing lines and interesting irregularities, has attracted the imagination of craftsmen since time began, lending itself to a seemingly endless variety of shapes. Today the preliminary steps in crafting wood are often performed with power tools such as the band saw *(page 86)*. But hand tools, as always, are indispensable for the finishing touches that give shaped wood its special beauty. The tools on these pages have been used for centuries, many of them essentially unchanged in design.

Hand tools for shaping wood fall into two general categories: cutting tools and scraping tools. In the first category are the drawknife, the forming tool, and many types of spokeshaves and planes; scraping tools include files, rasps and rifflers. Both types have advantages and disadvantages, and every woodworker eventually develops a battery of favorites. But a few general guidelines will help you choose the right tool for the job.

The greatest advantage of cutting tools is that they slice through wood, leaving a slick, smooth surface and a discernible grain. And because there are so many kinds of tools, you can find one to fit almost any situation. Drawknives, which are pulled toward the worker, and spokeshaves, which generally are pushed, can be used to curve edges, to shear the faces of narrow curved surfaces, even to smooth the inside of curved channels.

Planes, which are pushed, come in an astonishing array of shapes and sizes. The diminutive thumb plane fits easily into areas where planes with wider blades cannot go; the compass plane, with its flexible steel sole plate, molds itself to the contours of broad curved surfaces, both convex and concave. The forming tool, its cutting face covered with hundreds of tiny blades, is good for rounding off square corners.

The greatest disadvantage of the cutting tools is that they have a tendency to lift and break exposed grain ends as they cut. These tools cut most successfully when they are following the direction of the wood grain, which makes them particularly difficult to use in tight spots and on woods with irregular grains, such as bird's-eye maple.

Rasps, files and rifflers have tiny teeth that tear wood rather than cut it—this makes them convenient to use in any direction, regardless of grain. They are excellent tools for smoothing shaped surfaces and are invaluable in final finishing of intricately carved wood. However, they too have one disadvantage. In tearing the wood fibers, these tools—especially when they are coarse-surfaced—leave myriad tiny scratches that can obscure the grain pattern and dull the finished surface. This effect can be diminished by using a finer-toothed tool.

Caring for these cutting and scraping tools is simple but necessary. The blades of planes must be kept razor sharp; hone them with a whetstone. The teeth of rasps and files should be cleaned with a file card—a brush with soft wire bristles.

## Rough Shaping with a Drawknife

**Making a concave cut with a drawknife.** After outlining the cut on the wood and cutting away as much waste as possible with a band saw, clamp the stock in a vise, angling it slightly toward you. Lay the drawknife blade across the far end of the proposed cut, the cutting edge held bevel down. Tilt the blade slightly down and pull it toward you, making a shallow cut to the lowest point of the outline. As you pull, lift the tool handles to pry away wood chips. Repeat this initial cut, following the path of the outline and cutting more deeply into the wood each time. Keep cutting toward the low point until the resulting wood chips no longer break off easily. Then reverse the wood in the vise.

Cut the other side in the same way, working from the end toward the low point *(inset)*. As you near the low point, make shallow, slicing cuts, removing the wood in thin shavings to avoid breaking the grain on the first side of the cut.

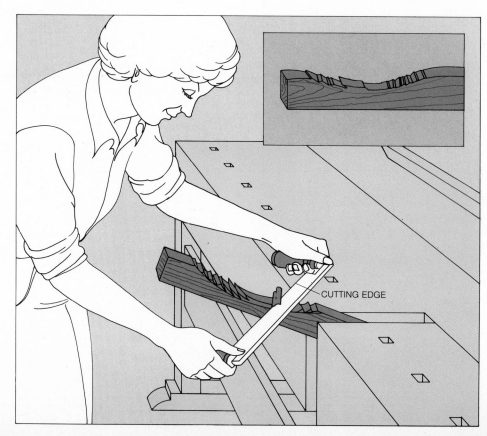

CUTTING EDGE

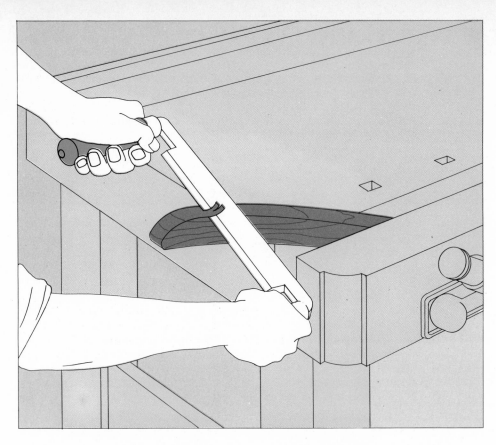

**Making a convex cut with a drawknife.** For a convex cut, begin at the high point of the curve and cut down and away from it; when both gradual and sharp curves are included in the design, as on the chair-back stile shown here, cut the sharper curve first. Hold the drawknife blade across the wood, bevel up and at approximately a 30° angle to the wood. Pull the blade toward you with shallow, shearing cuts that produce thin shavings. Continue cutting until the curve is the desired shape.

For the more gradual section of the curve, set the blade perpendicular to the wood and, again beginning at the high point of the curve, pull the knife toward you with shallow strokes until you have formed an even, continuous curve that meets the cut section. Then reverse the wood in the vise and cut the opposite end, starting as before at the high point of the curve.

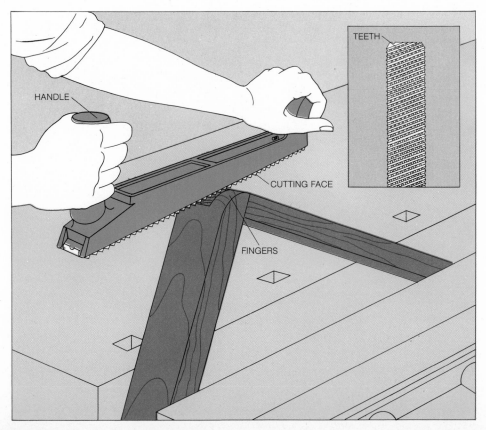

## Rounding a Corner with a Forming Tool

**Curving a right-angle joint.** Clamp the joint in a vise, pointed corner facing up. Hold the forming tool in both hands—one hand grasping the rear handle to push the tool, the other hand resting on the front of the tool to guide it. To round one side of the joint, hold the cutting face at an angle of about 5° to the wood surface facing you. Set the tool on the joint and, applying gentle steady pressure, push the cutting face halfway over the corner, ending the movement with the tool in a horizontal position. Make as many cuts as necessary to round half of the corner, then reverse the joint in the vise and repeat the cuts to shape the other side.

On a joint such as the finger joint shown here, where the grain direction changes abruptly, work slowly. The forming tool's teeth are arranged for a diagonal slicing cut (*inset*), designed to deal with varying grain directions, but sudden changes require deft and careful control.

# Versatile Spokeshaves for Smoothing Curves

**Making a rounded bevel on a curved edge.** After shaping the face of a curve with a drawknife (*page 94*), round its edges with a straight-bladed spokeshave. Grasp the spokeshave handles by resting your thumbs in the indented thumb rests on top of the handles and your index fingers on either side of the front, or nose, of the tool. With gentle pressure and repeated strokes, push the spokeshave along the edge of the curve, lifting thin shavings. Change the tilt of the tool with each stroke, to round the edge completely.

For a concave curve, like the one illustrated, work from the outer ends of the curve down toward its low point, to avoid lifting and breaking exposed grain ends. For a convex curve, work from the high point of the curve down toward its ends.

To adjust the spokeshave blade for these edge-smoothing cuts, set it to make as shallow a cut as possible. Loosen the thumbscrew on the covering cap, and turn the adjustment screws until the blade barely protrudes beyond the opening in the sole plate (*inset*). Tighten the thumbscrew.

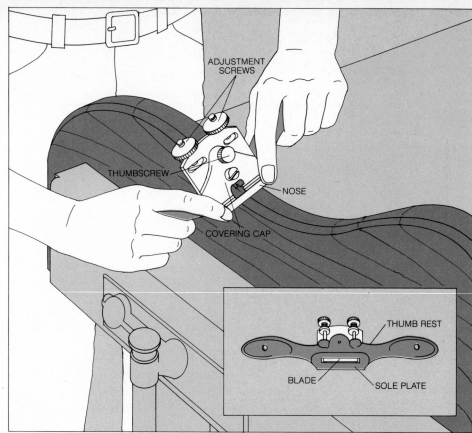

**Smoothing a wide, shallow channel.** Using a half-round spokeshave with a curved blade, grasp the handles by pressing your thumbs against the rear faces and wrapping your fingers around the front. Tilt the back of the spokeshave slightly toward you, set the edge of the blade in the channel and push the tool away from you with gentle, steady strokes. If the grain direction changes, reverse the tool, tilt the top away from you and pull the spokeshave toward you with the same stroking motion.

As with the straight-bladed spokeshave (*above*), adjust the half-round tool to make as shallow a cut as possible. Simply loosen the thumbscrew cap, releasing the blade and the covering cap, and move the blade into position by hand.

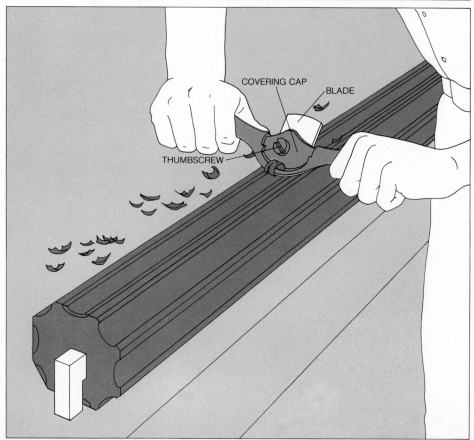

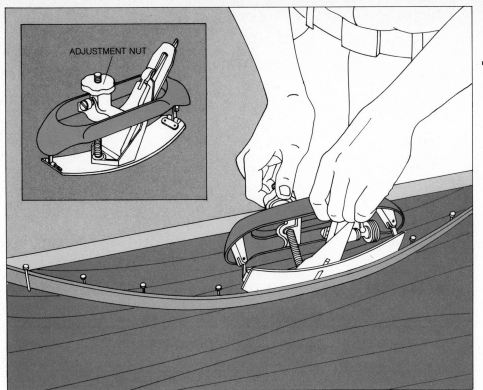

## A Flexible Plane That Follows Curved Surfaces

**1** **Adjusting the flexible sole plate.** First, establish the proposed curve by cutting a strip of ¾-inch lath to the desired length of the curve and setting it on edge between two nails driven into the face of the wood where the curve will begin and end. Wedge the lath between the nails, allowing it to form a smooth curve, then anchor the lath with supporting nails driven against the waste side of the curve at 5-inch intervals.

Use the curved lath as a guide for adjusting the sole plate of a compass plane. For a concave curve, as here, lay the plane on its side against the inside curve of the lath; turn the adjusting nut until the sole-plate curve is slightly sharper than the lath curve. For a convex curve, lay the plane on its side against the outside curve of the lath; adjust the sole plate to a curve slightly flatter than that of the lath. Then trace the outline of the lath on the wood, remove the lath and, using a band saw, rough-cut the curve to within ⅛ inch of the outline.

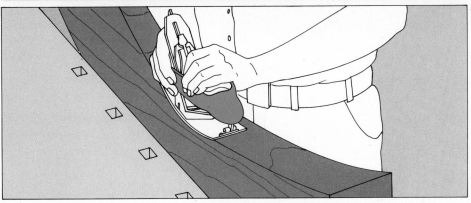

**2** **Smoothing the rough-cut curve.** Set the rough-cut wood in a vise. Grasp the back of the compass plane with one hand, guide the front with the other, and push the plane along the wood, following the penciled outline with long, smooth strokes. Work parallel with the direction of the grain, never across it or at an angle to it. For a concave cut, as here, start at the ends of the curve and move toward its low point; as you approach the low point, shorten your strokes to avoid tearing the exposed grain ends. For a convex curve, start at the high point of the curve and work down toward the ends.

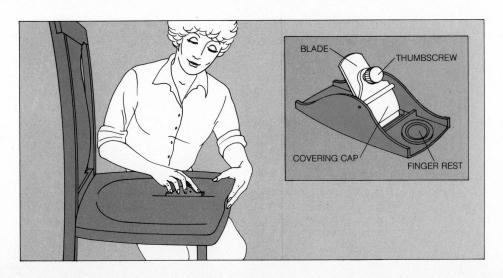

## A Tiny Plane for Tight Places

**Using a thumb plane.** Hold the thumb plane between your thumb and your index and middle fingers, with the index finger on the finger rest at the nose. Push down and forward with short, light strokes, guiding the tool with the index finger so that you are always working parallel with the grain.

Most of the smoothing done with a thumb plane requires a shallow cut. To adjust the blade, loosen the thumbscrew on the covering cap and set the blade to barely protrude beyond the opening in the sole plate (*inset*).

# Tools That Shape Wood by Scraping It

**A battery of rasps, files and rifflers.** Rasps and files have toothed scraping surfaces that are 6 to 12 inches long, with a tang at one end that fits snugly into a wooden handle. The scraping surface may take one of three forms: flat on both sides (as in these examples), round on one face and flat on the other, or completely round. The difference between them is that rasps, which have tiny individual teeth arranged in staggered rows, are generally used for rougher work; files, whose teeth are formed by long grooves cut at an angle across the tool face, are used for a smoother, finer finish. Both rasps and files come in varying degrees of coarseness, which is determined by the number of teeth per inch of scraping surface. The bastard-cut rasp shown here *(below, left)* has approximately 26 teeth per inch and is used for rough shaping of hard woods; for rough shaping of soft woods, a medium-cut rasp, which has about 36 teeth per inch, is used. A smooth-cut rasp has approximately 60 teeth per inch, set in an apparently random pattern; it produces more finished results. The single-cut file, which has grooves running in only one direction, and the more abrasive double-cut file, with crisscrossing grooves, are available in the same variety of coarseness designations as rasps are.

Rifflers *(below, right)* are double-ended tools with spatulate, curved or pointed heads; they are useful for cleaning intricately carved details and for shaping hard-to-reach spots. Their scraping surfaces are miniature versions of rasps and files, and they come in the same range of coarseness as rasps and files.

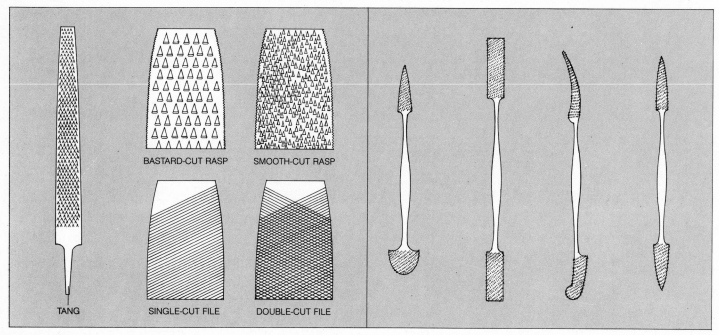

TANG     BASTARD-CUT RASP     SMOOTH-CUT RASP

SINGLE-CUT FILE     DOUBLE-CUT FILE

# Techniques for Using Scraping Tools

**Working with a rasp or a file.** Rasps and files are held in the same way—diagonally, with one hand on the handle to push the tool and the heel of the other hand resting on the front of the tool to guide it. Use a gentle forward stroke to scrape the wood; then lift the tool and move it backward to repeat the stroke, to avoid dulling the teeth. Depending on the results desired, rasps and files can be pushed in any direction along or across the grain. To finish and smooth a concave cut, as in this example, push the curved face of a half-round rasp down toward the low point of the curve, working diagonally across the grain with a gentle, upward stroke. For a convex shape, start at the high point of the curve and work down, using the flat side of the same tool and an up-and-over rocking motion diagonally across the grain of the wood.

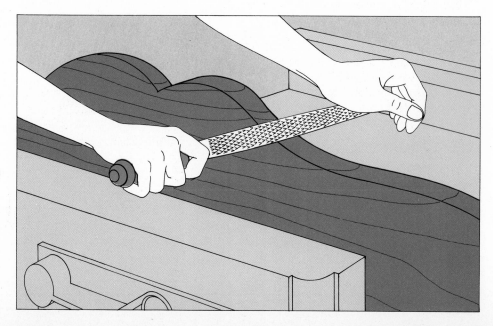

**Getting into tight confines with a riffler.** Pick a riffler to fit the cut—in this example a curved riffler is used to smooth a narrow, routed channel outlining the edge of a table apron. Hold the riffler in one hand, using the index finger of that hand and the thumb of the other hand to guide the tool as you push it. Never pull the riffler back along its path; lift it up from the work and reposition it to repeat the smoothing cut.

## A Chair Shaped Completely with Hand Tools

From the top of its curving backrest to the bottoms of its mock-claw feet, the contours of the chair shown here were smoothed and refined with hand-held shaping tools. The concave and convex profile of the backrest *(top inset)* was cut first on a band saw *(page 86);* then the gentle curves were shaped with a spokeshave, the sharper curves with a file. The broad shallow curves of the front and back faces of the backrest were shaped with the flexible sole plate of a compass plane. A jig saw was used to rough-cut the harp-shaped splat *(page 93);* then the edges were smoothed with a spokeshave and a riffler, the latter taking care of the tight spots.

On the gently contoured seat of the chair *(middle inset),* a forming tool established the shape; a thumb plane was then used to refine it. The curved edges of the seat were smoothed with a smooth-cut rasp. The long curves of the stiles and legs were rough-cut first on a band saw and then were shaped with a drawknife. The final smoothing was accomplished with a spokeshave. The smaller, deeply incised curves of the mock-claw feet *(bottom inset)* were carved out first with a drawknife, then smoothed with rifflers.

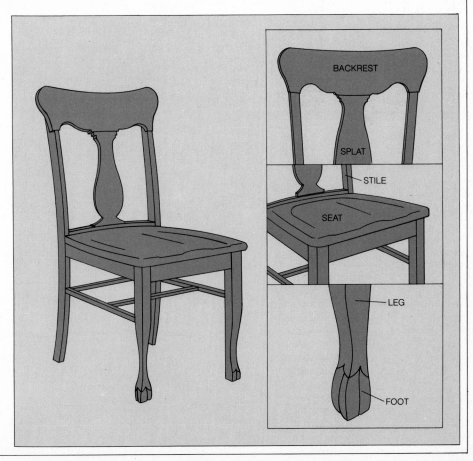

# Wood-Turning with a Lathe

Although electricity has replaced the woodworker's apprentice as the power that drives a woodworking lathe, the combination of whirling wood and hand-held carving tools continues to be the preferred method for creating certain kinds of elaborate symmetrical shapes—stair balusters, drawer pulls, newel-post caps and other architectural trim, not to mention furniture legs and wooden bowls. The idea of turning wood to shape it, known to artisans of the earliest civilizations, has never outlived its usefulness and has appealed to craftsmen ever since.

To a woodturner, strength is not nearly as important as finesse. Developing a relaxed stance and a proper tool grip are the first steps to accomplish in using a lathe. Once these are mastered and you begin to feel the interplay between the spinning wood and the cutting edges of the tools, learning the techniques of turning becomes easier.

There are only two basic methods of shaping wood mounted on a lathe—cutting and scraping. Cutting, with the hand tool held at various angles to shave away waste wood layer by layer, is the more traditional method. This technique is more difficult to master than scraping—it takes time to develop a feel for holding the tool at the proper angle—but cutting produces results that are smoother and more professional.

In scraping, the tool is pushed straight into the wood as it spins; the tool edge, instead of shearing away thin shavings, scrapes away small particles of wood. Scraping leaves a rougher finish on the wood than cutting does.

Selecting the right wood for turning is as important as developing proper techniques. Hardwoods generally are better than softwoods, and close-grained hardwoods such as maple, birch, ash and cherry all produce smooth, crisp-looking results. An open-grained hardwood such as oak is less satisfactory, since it tends to splinter. A softwood such as pine is difficult to turn in intricate shapes, but it is inexpensive and useful for practicing. No matter what wood you choose, be sure that it is free of splits and knots. Tool edges catch on such imperfections, and the resulting chips and breaks can ruin a piece of work.

The size of the piece of wood you can turn is determined by the size of your lathe. A typical home-shop lathe will hold a narrow piece of wood, called a spindle, up to 32 inches in length, or a block of wood that has a diagonal measurement of up to 10 inches.

Keeping a lathe in good working order requires little time and effort. Oil the moving parts according to the manufacturer's instructions, and be sure to keep the tool free of waste wood that could clog the machinery.

Wood-turning hand tools require more care. Keep the cutting edges sharp by honing them on a fine oilstone. Set the bevel of the tool flat on the stone and, with gentle pressure, push the blade around in a figure-8 pattern. For a curved bevel such as the one on a gouge *(center, opposite page),* rock the bevel from side to side as you push it through the figure 8. A few strokes with a slipstone will finish off the inside of a gouge's curved cutting edge.

**The anatomy of a wood lathe.** Wood that is spun on a lathe is supported between two end parts called the headstock and the tailstock. The headstock is permanently mounted at the left end of the lathe base, called its bed; the tailstock slides along this bed so that the tool can accommodate wood of various lengths.

The headstock spindle, which turns the wood, holds a part called the center, which has spurs or screws that penetrate the wood; this driving spindle is powered by a motor. Pulleys on the motor and on the lathe, connected by a belt, provide several speeds. On the model shown, the way to control the speed is to move the belt from one level to another on two stepped pulleys, one on the motor and the other inside the headstock. The large exposed wheel on the headstock makes it possible to turn the work by hand. The spindle of the tailstock holds the cup center; it does not rotate the wood, but it can be moved in and out with a second handwheel, to ensure that the wood is tightly mounted on the lathe.

Between the headstock and the tailstock is a tool rest; it can be moved along the bed and adjusted to various heights and angles. It supports the various cutting and scraping tools *(opposite)* that are used to shape the wood.

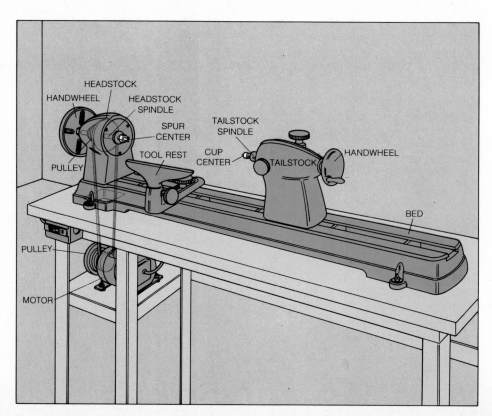

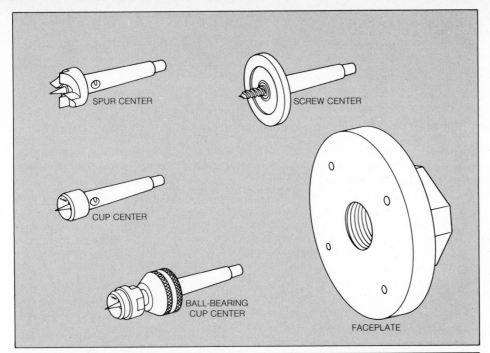

SPUR CENTER

SCREW CENTER

CUP CENTER

BALL-BEARING
CUP CENTER

FACEPLATE

**Locking the wood in a lathe.** Five basic spindle centers for holding wood in a lathe are detailed here. The spur center, which spins the wood as well as holding it, has four sharp spurs that are embedded in the headstock end of the wood. The cup center remains stationary in the tailstock spindle; it has a concave end, so only the thin rim and the point penetrate the spinning wood. An alternative center for use with the tailstock spindle is a cup center with ball bearings that permit it to spin freely as the wood turns, thus reducing friction.

Some lathe work, such as that involved in shaping a wooden bowl, requires that the wood be attached only to the headstock. This work is done with the faceplate—a metal disc that screws onto the headstock spindle. The wood is attached to the faceplate with screws; such faceplates range from 3 to 10 inches in diameter, the size determined by the size of the wood block being shaped. The screw center is used for smaller faceplate turnings, such as drawer pulls.

CUTTING
EDGE

BLADE

BEVEL

GOUGE

PARTING TOOL

SKEW CHISEL

ROUNDNOSE CHISEL

DIAMOND-POINT CHISEL

SQUARENOSE CHISEL

**Lathe tools for cutting and scraping.** The gouge, the parting tool and the skew chisel are cutting tools. The gouge has a curved blade with a rounded cutting edge that is beveled on the convex side. Gouges range in width from ¼ inch to 1 inch or even more. They are used for reducing rectangular stock to a cylindrical shape and for cutting grooves and coves. The parting tool has two flat sides; its two bevels are angled toward each other to form a narrow cutting edge at the end of the blade. When it is held so that the bevels are vertical, the parting tool is used for making narrow grooves of any desired

depth. A skew chisel has a cutting edge that is ground at an angle to the side of the blade. This kind of chisel is used for cutting beads, V grooves and tapers.

Roundnose, diamond-point and squarenose chisels are scraping tools rather than cutting tools. They have flat blades of various shapes and are beveled on one side. Although scraping tools are not positioned in the same way as cutting tools, they can be used to create some of the same shapes. They are also used extensively for faceplate turning *(page 112)*.

## Safety Rules for Lathe Use

In addition to applying the safety rules listed for all power tools *(page 9)*, take the following precautions when you operate a lathe:

☐ Before starting the lathe, be sure that the wood is well anchored at both ends and that all surfaces will clear the tool rest as the wood spins.

☐ As you turn and shape the wood, stop the lathe periodically and readjust the tool rest to keep it about ¼ inch from the wood you are working.

☐ Use a speed chart *(page 102)* to determine a safe turning speed for each project; never operate the lathe faster than the speed recommended. If you have difficulty controlling the hand tool you are using, reduce the speed.

# Hand Positions for Holding Lathe Tools

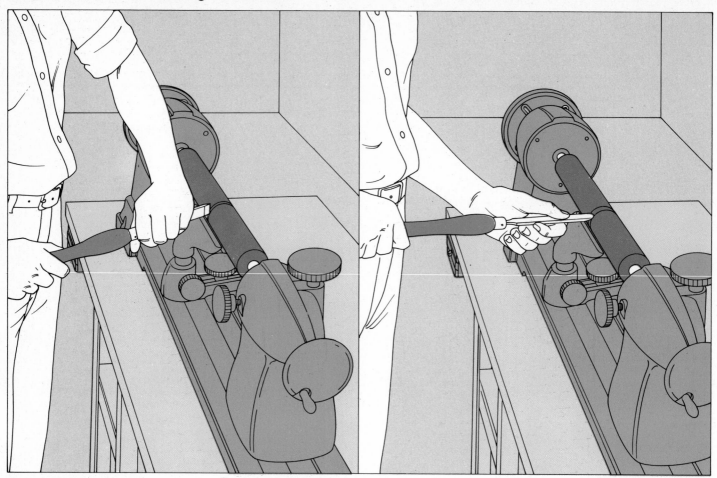

**Holding the tool as the wood turns.** Although the lathe tools used for cutting and for scraping perform different functions, they are all held in the same way. Grip the end of the tool handle firmly but not tightly with one hand, keeping your forearm close to your body. This arm directs the action of the tool. Hold the tool's blade lightly against the tool rest with the other hand. This hand may be positioned with four fingers on top of the blade and the thumb below it, with the little finger touching the tool rest (*above, left*). Or you may prefer to put the thumb on top and four fingers below, with the index finger against the tool rest (*above, right*).

With a cutting tool, such as a skew chisel (*above, left*), hold the bevel against the stock and the blade, angled for the desired cut, atop the tool rest. As the wood spins, raise the handle gradually in the direction of the cut, driving the cutting edge into the wood. Here the skew chisel is being used to cut a V groove.

With a scraping tool, such as a roundnose chisel (*above, right*), hold the blade horizontal across the tool rest, with the bevel down, and feed the cutting edge straight into the wood. Here the roundnose chisel is being used to cut a groove.

## Setting Turning Speeds to Suit the Job

| Diameter of work | LATHE SPEEDS (revolutions per minute) | | |
| --- | --- | --- | --- |
| | Roughing cut | Shaping cut | Finishing cut and sanding |
| less than 2'' | 900-1,400 | 2,200-2,800 | 3,000-4,200 |
| 2''–4'' | 600-1,000 | 1,800-2,400 | 2,400-3,400 |
| 4''–6'' | 600-1,000 | 1,200-1,800 | 1,800-2,400 |
| 6''–8'' | 400-800 | 800-1,200 | 1,200-1,800 |
| 8''–10'' | 300-700 | 700-1,000 | 1,000-1,200 |
| more than 10'' | 300-600 | 600-900 | 600-900 |

**Choosing the best speed.** Recommended lathe-turning speeds are listed in this table, expressed in revolutions per minute. First match the diameter of the stock you are using with the dimensions in the left column of the table; in general, the thicker the stock, the slower it must be turned. Then at the top of the table find the type of work you want to do. Slow speeds are the best for faceplate turning and for shaping rectangular stock into a cylinder. Medium speeds are used for cutting various shapes once you have a cylinder. The fastest speeds are used for the final smoothing and sanding. Unusually narrow or long stock may vibrate at the recommended speed; if this happens, try the next lower speed. A lathe with four-step pulley wheels (*page 100*) may not run at exactly the recommended speed; if so, use the closest slower speed.

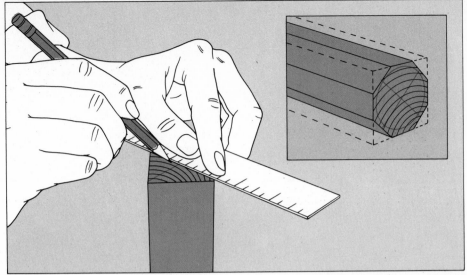

## Mounting the Wood in the Machine

**1 Finding the centers.** After you cut the stock to the desired length on a table saw and carefully square the sides, draw diagonal lines from corner to corner on both ends to locate their centers precisely. On what will become the headstock end, use a handsaw to cut a kerf ⅛ inch deep along each diagonal line.

If the stock is more than 2 inches square, use a compass to scribe the largest possible circle on one end of the stock. Then set a table-saw blade at a 45° angle, and bevel the edges of the stock, starting each of the four cuts just outside the scribed circle (*inset*).

**2 Embedding the spur center.** With the spur center removed from the headstock spindle, set its point at the intersection of the diagonal saw kerfs, with the spurs positioned over the kerfs. Use a wooden mallet to tap the shank of the spur center lightly, until the spurs are firmly embedded in the wood.

Push the cup-center shank onto the tailstock spindle and lubricate its center point with soap or wax. Turn the tailstock handwheel to retract the spindle as far as possible into the tailstock.

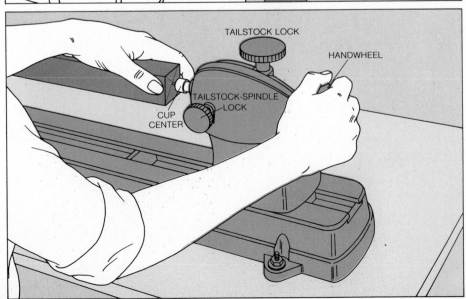

**3 Fastening the wood in the lathe.** Loosen the tailstock lock so that you can slide the tailstock assembly along the bed away from the headstock. Push the spur-center shank into the headstock spindle and, as you support the wood with one hand, push the tailstock toward the wood until the point of the cup center nearly touches the wood. Fasten the tailstock in this position with the tailstock lock.

Turn the tailstock handwheel to drive the cup-center point into the wood at the intersection of the diagonal pencil lines, until the rim of the cup center penetrates the wood. Finally, use the tailstock-spindle lock to fix the cup center in this position. Give the stock a spin by hand; if it wobbles or does not turn freely, readjust the tailstock spindle.

If the wood has not been beveled with a table saw, shave off its edges with a small plane before you begin rounding them with lathe tools.

# From Square Stock to Perfectly Round Cylinder

**1** **Rough cutting with a lathe gouge.** Slide the tool rest all the way to the right and set it level with the midpoint of the wood being turned, ⅛ to ¼ inch from touching it. Turn on the lathe and place a large gouge on the tool rest, 2 inches in from the right end of the wood, keeping the handle angled slightly downward and the concave face of the gouge blade turned toward the right but not vertical. Push the gouge forward until the bevel touches the wood. Then, holding the gouge firmly, raise the tool handle slightly until the cutting edge shears the wood. Making light cuts, slide the blade in a straight line to the right until it passes off the end of the spinning wood. Repeat the shearing motion until you have rounded the section.

Until the wood becomes cylindrical, it will tend to splinter and vibrate. If splintering is excessive, reduce the lathe speed and make shallower cuts.

When the first section of the stock has been rounded, cut successive 2-inch sections the same way, progressing from right to left along the stock but always cutting from left to right. Turn off the lathe and adjust the position of the tool rest when necessary, to keep it close to the work. Leave the last 2-inch section at the left uncut.

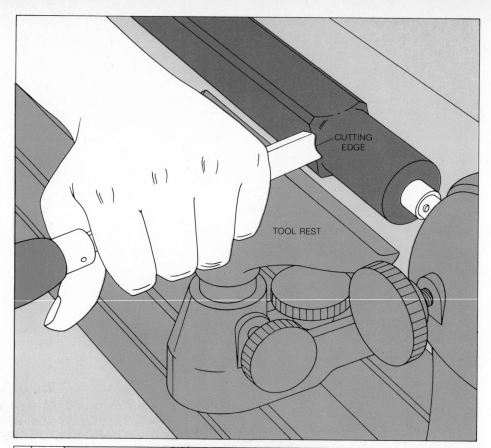

**2** **Rounding the last section.** To shape the last 2-inch section of the cylinder at the left end, turn the gouge over so that the concave face of the blade faces left. Round off the cylinder as before, but this time cut from right to left until the blade passes off the end of the wood.

To be sure the cylinder is evenly rounded, make a continuous cut from left to right along its entire length. Stop the lathe to move or adjust the tool rest whenever necessary.

**3** **Final smoothing with a skew chisel.** Set the tool rest ¼ inch from the wood at the left end of the cylinder, turn on the lathe, and place a skew chisel on the tool rest 2 inches in from the end of the wood (*below, top*). Angle the handle downward and hold the blade at a 25° to 30° angle to the cylinder. Push forward so that the bevel touches the wood, but keep the skew point clear of the wood to avoid gashes. Hold the blade lightly against the cylinder and slide it to the left, directing the lower half of the cutting edge so that you feel very little resistance and so that the cut produces very thin shavings. Push the blade off the end of the stock.

Reverse the blade position (*below, bottom*) and cut in the same manner from left to right along the entire length of the cylinder, moving the tool rest when necessary. Repeat the cuts until the cylinder is perfectly smooth.

## A Shapely Leg That Sums Up the Repertoire of a Lathe

**Four basic shapes cut with a lathe.** One unusual furniture leg displays the four commonest shapes that can be produced on a lathe. These shapes can be cut in any number and in any order to produce a variety of patterns. A bead is a rounded shape cut with a skew chisel. A taper is wider at one end than at the other and usually is an elongated shape; it is cut with a parting tool, a gouge and a skew chisel. Rectangular sections can be left uncut, except for shoulders, which are rounded with a skew chisel. A cove is a concave section, with equal diameters at the ends and a smaller diameter in the middle; this shape is cut with a parting tool and a gouge.

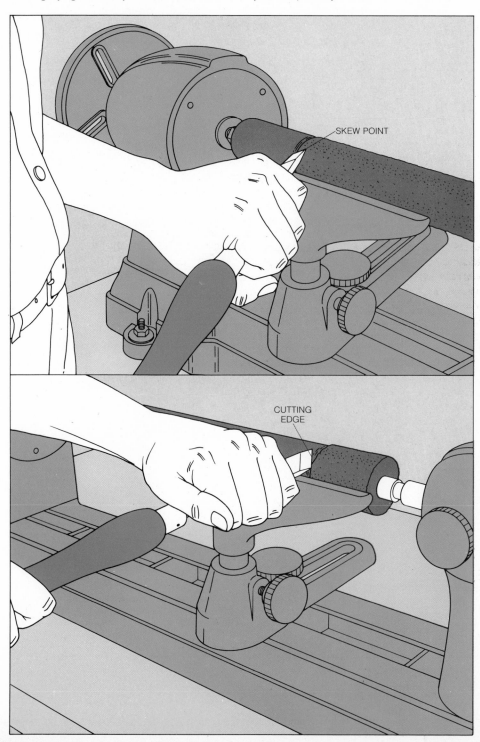

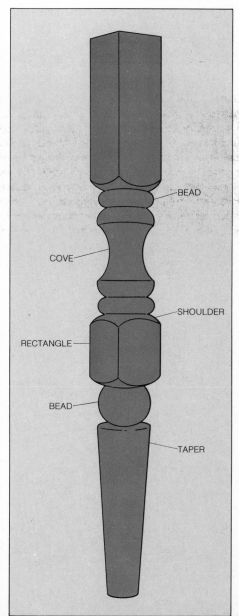

# Raising a Bead

**1** **Making end grooves with a skew.** Set the tool rest slightly above the center of the cylindrical stock and about ¼ inch from it. Switch on the lathe, and mark the sides of the bead by holding a pencil lightly in two places against the spinning cylinder. If the bead will be wider than ½ inch, add a third guideline midway between the first two lines drawn.

Place a skew chisel on the tool rest, with the blade on edge and the skew point down. Tilt the tool handle very slightly downward, to make certain the cut will be made just above the midpoint of the stock. Push the skew point straight into the stock at a side guideline, scraping a V-shaped groove ⅛ inch deep. Cut a groove at the other side guideline in the same way, but do not cut into the center guideline.

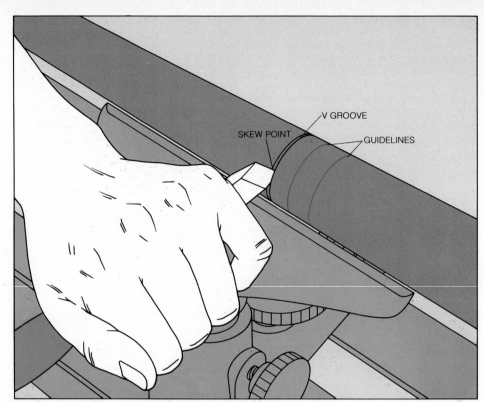

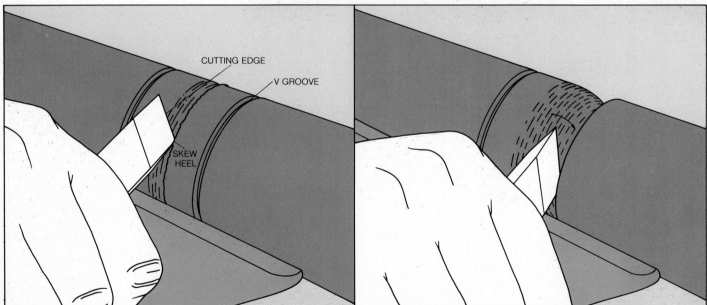

**2** **Shaping the bead.** With the stock spinning, place the blade of the skew chisel almost flat on the tool rest at the center of the bead. Position the heel of the cutting edge to the right of and lower than the point, with the tool handle angled slightly downward. Push the blade forward until the skew's bevel, but not its cutting edge, touches the wood at the center guideline *(above, left)*. To begin the cut, raise and twist the handle slightly until the bottom half of the cutting edge just shears the wood. Then, in one continuous motion, roll the heel of the blade toward

the right groove, raising the handle and pushing the blade forward into the wood as the chisel turns. End with the skew's cutting edge vertical in the groove, the heel down *(above, right)*. To make the groove deeper for a rounder bead, push the heel of the cutting edge farther into the groove before withdrawing the blade.

Cut the other side of the bead in the same way, but start with the heel of the cutting edge pointing to the left. Alternate right and left cuts until the bead is the desired shape.

## Incising a Cove

**1 Cutting the V grooves.** Set the tool rest even with the center of the stock and ¼ inch from it; turn on the lathe, and mark the sides and center of the cove on the spinning stock with a pencil. Then place a skew chisel almost on its edge on the tool rest, point up, in line with a side guideline. Hold the blade so that you angle the heel of the cutting edge slightly toward the center of the planned cove. Keeping the tool handle angled slightly downward, push the skew's heel into the wood to form an angled V groove ⅛ inch deep. For a similar V groove at the other side of the cove, angle the blade in the opposite direction so that the heel again points toward the center of the cove; make the second cut *(inset)*.

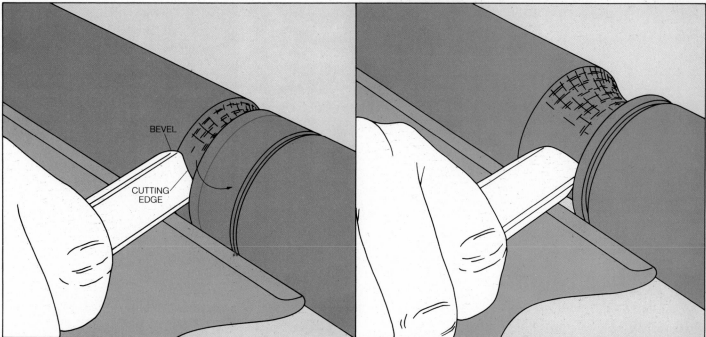

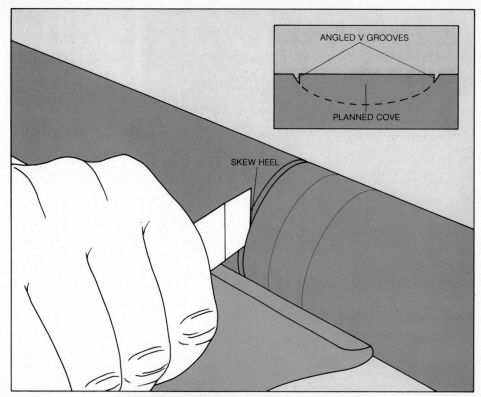

**2 Shaping the cove with a gouge.** Position a gouge almost on its edge atop the tool rest, holding it so that its bevel rests against a V groove and its concave side faces toward the center of the cove. Angle the cutting edge slightly toward the cove center, the tool handle slightly down and away from it *(above, left)*. Push the cutting edge into the stock and, in one continuous motion, raise the tool handle slightly to push the cutting edge into the wood while rolling the bevel down and toward the center of the cove *(above, right)*. End the cut with the blade horizontal, the bevel down, at the center of the cove. Be sure that you do not cut past the center.

Cut the other side of the cove in the same way, but start with the bevel, cutting edge and tool handle angled in the opposite direction. Continue to make similar cuts in alternating directions until the cove is the desired shape.

# Creating a Taper

**1 Sizing the taper ends.** Smooth the stock to make a cylinder *(page 104)* ⅛ inch greater in diameter than the wide end of the planned taper. Then set the tool rest just above the center of the stock and ¼ inch from it, turn on the lathe, and mark the ends of the taper with a pencil. If the taper will be longer than 8 inches, mark its center as well. Starting at the wide end of the taper, place a parting tool on edge on the tool rest, the lower bevel of the cutting edge against the stock, the tool handle angled slightly downward. Raise the handle to drive the cutting edge into the stock.

Stop the lathe frequently so that you can check the depth of the narrow cut, using calipers set to the desired diameter *(inset)*. The cut is completed when both points of the calipers slide easily onto the wood inside the groove. Then cut and measure a groove at the narrow end of the taper in the same manner.

To establish the diameter needed for a middle groove in a taper longer than 8 inches, add the diameters of the end grooves and divide by two.

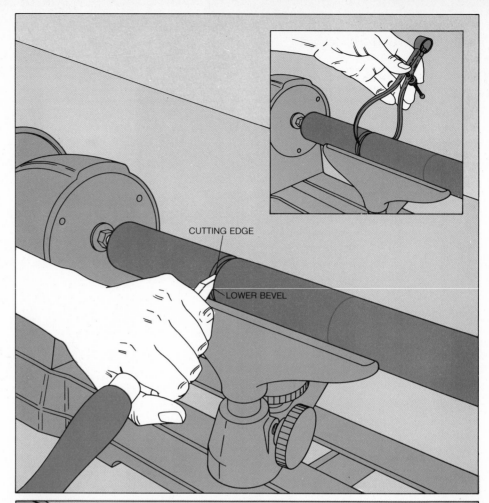

CUTTING EDGE

LOWER BEVEL

**2 Cutting the taper.** Starting at the groove that marks the wide end of the taper, cut along the entire length of the taper with a large gouge. Use the technique described for rough-cutting a cylinder *(page 104)*, but gradually apply greater forward pressure along the length of the cut so that you remove more wood as you approach the narrow end. Repeat the same cutting motion until you have reached the desired diameter at both ends of the taper. Stop the lathe periodically and hold a straightedge against the wood, to be sure there are no unwanted bulges.

Use a skew chisel in one continuous cut to smooth the surface of the taper *(page 105)*.

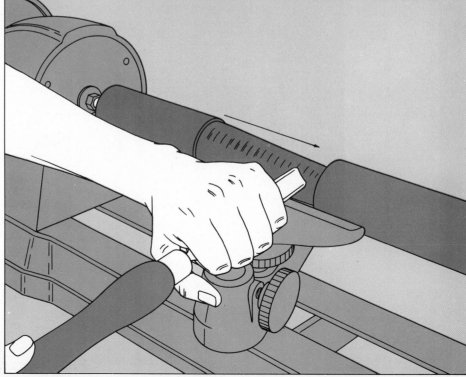

# A Rectangular Section
# with Rounded Shoulders

**1 Marking off the rectangle.** After you have
squared an entire length of stock with a table saw
and have planed or sanded the surfaces smooth,
use a pencil and a combination square to mark
the ends of any section that will remain square after the turning is completed. Mark both ends
of the section on all four faces of the stock. In the
example shown in the drawing below, the rectangle is at the end of the piece of stock, so only
one set of pencil lines is necessary. Mount the
stock on the lathe as described on page 103, but
do not bevel the edges with a plane.

**2 Cutting a groove.** Set the tool rest at the center of the stock, making sure that the edges of
the spinning stock will clear the tool rest by
¼ inch. Turn on the lathe and set a skew chisel,
point down, on the tool rest, with the handle
angled slightly downward. Push the skew point
straight into the wood at the guideline. Then
roll the tool handle alternately to the left and the
right, opening up the cut to form a V groove
about ½ inch wide. Apply forward pressure until
the point starts to cut all around the stock.
Make the same cut at any other guidelines.

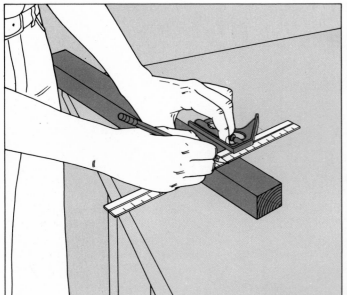

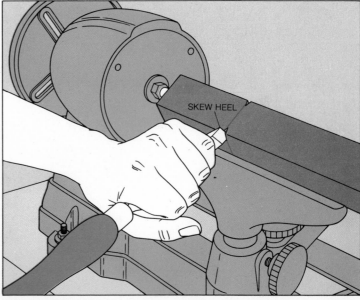

**3 Rounding the shoulders.** With the wood still
spinning, position the skew chisel on the tool rest
in line with the V groove, the skew point on top
and angled toward the rectangular section. The
cutting edge should be almost horizontal, the
skew point well above the spinning corners so that
it does not catch and chip the stock. Push the
blade forward and, with a motion similar to the
one used to cut the side of a bead (*page 106*),
raise the tool handle with a steady pressure to
direct the cutting edge into the wood as you
roll the heel of the cutting edge down into the
V groove, ending the motion with the cutting
edge in a vertical position. Repeat the cut until
the shoulder is fully rounded.

If you want to cut a deeper shoulder, use a
gouge to remove the excess stock that is adjacent
to the shoulder (*page 104*).

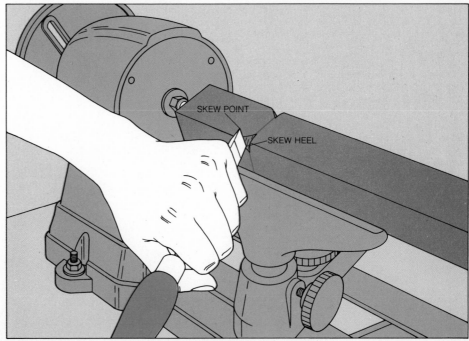

# Using a Template to Plan and Turn a Spindle

**1** **Making the template.** Draw an outline of the proposed design parallel to and about 2 inches from the edge of a sheet of heavy paper. Use a ruler to measure the diameters of the breaks—the high and low points of every shape in the design. As you measure each break, draw a line from it to the edge of the paper; on each line, note the diameter of the shape at that point. Note the diameter at the midpoint of any taper longer than 8 inches. When you are duplicating the shape of an existing piece of turned wood, use calipers to measure the break diameters and the spacing between breaks. Then transfer the measurements to the paper.

Glue the paper pattern to a piece of ⅛-inch hardboard, lining up the paper edge with the hardboard edge. To make the template—actually a reverse pattern of the design—cut along the pattern edge nearest the edge of the hardboard *(inset)*, using a band saw. Then smooth the curves and grooves of the template with a file.

Mount your stock in the lathe and turn it to a cylinder, except in the sections that are projected to remain rectangular *(page 109)*.

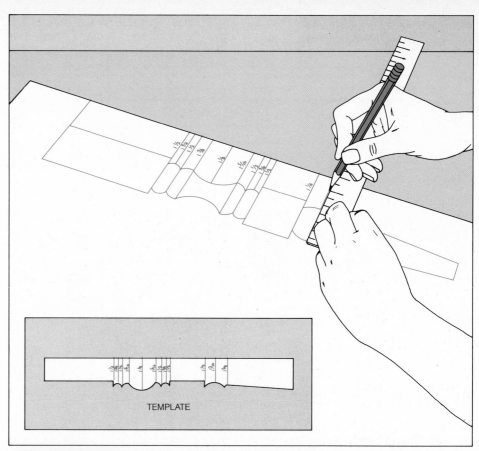

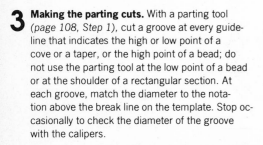

TEMPLATE

**2** **Marking guidelines on the wood.** With the lathe at rest, hold the straight edge of the template against the stock and, at the end of each break line, make a pencil mark on the cylinder. Then remove the template, place the pencil on the tool rest with the point against a mark and rotate the wood by hand to draw a guideline completely around the cylinder. Repeat this procedure at every break point.

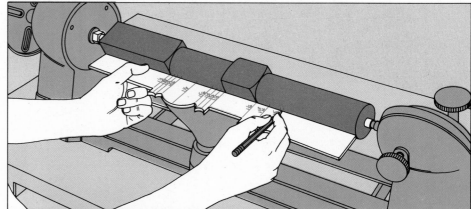

**3** **Making the parting cuts.** With a parting tool *(page 108, Step 1)*, cut a groove at every guideline that indicates the high or low point of a cove or a taper, or the high point of a bead; do not use the parting tool at the low point of a bead or at the shoulder of a rectangular section. At each groove, match the diameter to the notation above the break line on the template. Stop occasionally to check the diameter of the groove with the calipers.

When all the grooves have been cut to the correct depth, begin to shape the cylinder, using the tools and cutting techniques on pages 104-105.

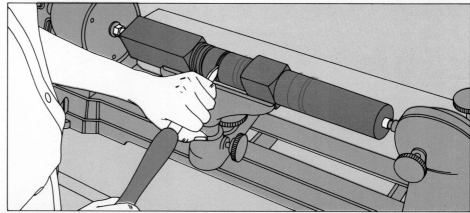

**4** **Using the template to check your work.** As you shape the cylinder, stop the lathe periodically and hold the cut edge of the template against your work, noting which sections need additional cutting. The shaping is complete when the template fits snugly against the spindle, with no gaps between the template and the wood.

## Smoothing Shaped Wood on a Spinning Lathe

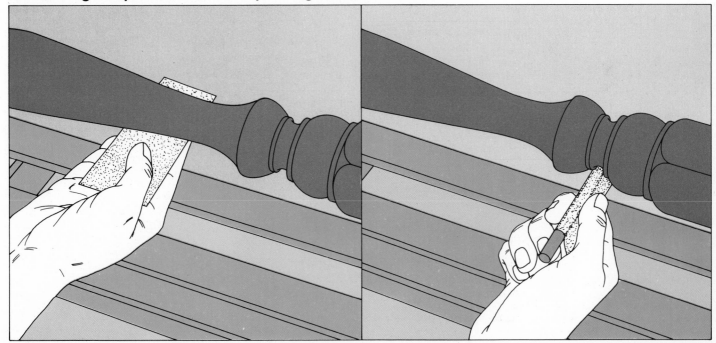

**Sanding the spinning stock.** To smooth an elongated shape like the taper at left above, fold a piece of 120- to 180-grit sandpaper in thirds, to a width of about 2 inches. Turn on the lathe and hold the paper underneath the spinning stock, pressing lightly and moving steadily back

and forth along the shape to avoid sanding away too much wood in one spot. Repeat the procedure with 220- to 280-grit paper.

To smooth a narrower shape, such as a V groove or a small cove (*right, above*), just wrap the

piece of sandpaper around a dowel or a wedge that fits the shape, and hold the paper below the stock as it spins on the lathe. Press the sandpaper lightly against the wood, taking care not to rub away the definition of the shape. Progress to a finer grade of sandpaper, as above.

# Turning Wood on a Faceplate

Wood-turning on a faceplate—that is, with the wood anchored at only one end of the lathe—is popular among woodworkers who have an eye for exotic grains and a penchant for designing bowls, doorknobs and newel-post caps in unusual shapes.

Some lathes have special features for faceplate turning. On a gap-bed lathe, part of the bed next to the headstock is cut away to leave extra room for a large piece of wood. On some other lathes, the headstock is equipped for outboard turning, which allows the wood to be fastened to either the outer or the inner face of the headstock. But an ordinary lathe will shape the face of a piece of wood up to about 8 inches in diameter—wide enough to accommodate a doorknob or the newel-post cap that is shown on these pages.

Faceplates that screw onto the headstock spindle and anchor the spinning wood *(page 101, top)* are available in several sizes; choose one about ½ inch smaller in diameter than the base of the piece that you are planning to turn. The screws that are used to fasten the wood to the faceplate should be as long as possible—up to 2 inches. But be sure they will not extend into a part of the wood that will be cut away.

Although cutting tools may be used to round the sides of the wood as it is being turned on a faceplate, the shaping is generally done with scraping tools. Scraping *(page 102, right)* allows more control over the tool and the spinning stock than cutting allows. The extra control is necessary because the pieces of wood are wider. Scraping is also the preferred method for the shaping of end grain, an integral part of faceplate turning.

Wood is prepared for faceplate turning much as it is for spindle turning *(page 103, Step 1)*. First square the piece on a table saw, then plane the surface that will be fastened to the faceplate. Draw diagonal lines from corner to corner on the planed surface, to locate the center point of the wood. Then use a compass to swing a circle from the center point, ⅛ inch larger than the largest diameter of the finished piece. Use a band saw to trim away excess wood around the outside of the circle.

## Mounting and Turning a Newel-Post Cap

**1** **Fastening the stock to the faceplate.** Position the faceplate on the planed surface of the stock, aligning the threaded center hole of the faceplate with the center point on the wood. With a pencil, mark the faceplate screw-hole locations on the wood. Drill pilot holes, and screw the faceplate to the stock. Then screw the faceplate to the headstock spindle on the lathe.

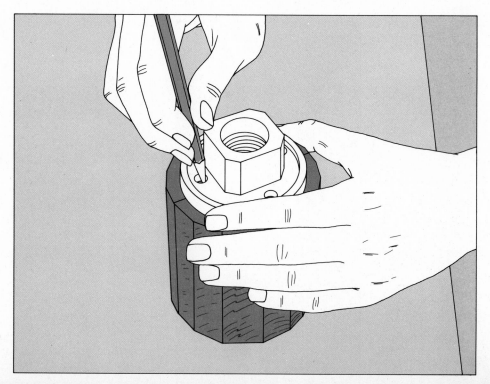

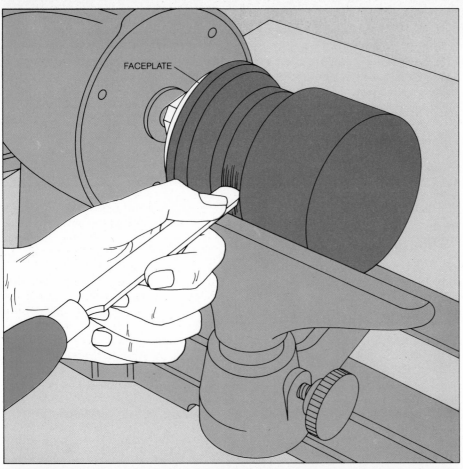

FACEPLATE

**2** **Shaping the sides of the cap.** Smooth the wood to a cylinder *(page 104, Steps 1 and 2)*, and use a roundnose chisel to shape the sides of the cap. For a cove shape, set the chisel on the tool rest at the planned center of the cap, hold the tool in the scraping position *(page 102, right)*, bevel edge down, and press the cutting edge straight into the spinning wood to make a preliminary groove. Widen the groove to the desired cove shape by repeating the same scraping procedure on both sides of the first groove, sliding the chisel toward the center of the cove and increasing the forward pressure as you go.

To form a bead shape, use a squarenose chisel in the same pivoting motion described in Step 3, below, forming first one side, then the other.

**3** **Rounding the end of the cap.** To shape end grain into a convex dome, set the tool rest at about a 45° angle to the center line of the stock and ¼ inch from the wood. Rest a squarenose chisel on the tool rest in the scraping position, bevel down, and push the left corner of the cutting edge into the spinning wood to scrape a shallow groove. Then gradually slide the blade along the tool rest, pivoting the cutting edge in a gentle arc toward the center of the stock. Do not move the tool past the center of the stock. Repeat the scraping motion until the wood is the desired shape, stopping to readjust the tool rest whenever necessary.

Form a groove or a dishlike depression in the end grain with a roundnose chisel, using the scraping technique in Step 2, above.

# High-speed Sanders That Smooth Many Shapes

Many woodworking projects are simpler to finish if the parts are sanded before they are assembled. Two kinds of power sanders make quick work of this step. A combination belt-and-disk sander smooths flat surfaces and most curved and irregular surfaces; an inflatable tubular sander, used with a portable power drill, handles inside curves and compound curves with dispatch.

The continuous abrasive belt of the combination sander stretches across two rotating drums and can be oriented for the job at hand. Set horizontally, it is especially useful for sanding parallel to the grain and for sanding long boards; if the boards are wider than the belt, they are sanded in repeated passes. Set vertically, the belt is useful for sanding the ends of wide boards, such as those used

to construct deep drawers. By removing some of the guard plates on the belt sander, changing the belt tension or adding specially made forms, you can adapt it for working on a variety of curved and elongated surfaces.

The disk sander, the other component of this combination tool, is best suited to sanding end grain on smaller pieces of wood; it is also useful for smoothing miter cuts, bevels and outside curves, such as the edge of a wooden disk.

Except when sanding with a template *(page 117)*, it is essential to keep the work moving continuously over a belt sander. Power sanding removes a great deal of wood so quickly that holding the work in one place for more than a moment can flatten a curve or put a dimple into a flat surface. Movement also helps

keep the abrasive surface from clogging.

Routine care for the sander includes inspecting the abrasive surface frequently and, with the machine turned off, brushing clogged areas clean. Replace a frayed belt; it could cause injury if it breaks while in use. Check the abrasive disk for fraying and for loose adhesive, which might cause the disk to fly off the spinning metal base.

Check the tension and tracking of the belt periodically. For most jobs the correct tension is one that keeps the belt stiff when it is pressed; to adjust the tension, change the distance between the two drums. A correctly tracking belt remains centered on both drums; to adjust tracking, tilt the axis of the idler drum slightly. The way to tilt the idler drum varies on different brands of sanders.

**A combination belt-and-disk sander.** This shop tool is essentially two machines in one, sharing a motor. The belt sander has a continuous strip of abrasive-coated fabric, usually 4 to 6 inches wide. The belt rotates over two drums—the drive drum, turned by the motor, and the idler drum, which turns freely. Handles and knobs on the sides of the unit are used to change the position of the idler drum for adjusting the tracking and tension of the belt. The unit tilts from vertical to horizontal locking at any point on a 90° arc, by means of nuts located on the side of the drive drum. Normally the belt is covered by a back plate, a side guard and an idler-drum guard; all three can be removed for special sanding jobs, by means of either locking nuts or knobs.

The disk sander, attached to the motor shaft, is a metal plate to which an abrasive-coated disk is glued. Worktables for the belt and the disk can be tilted and locked at any angle from 90° to 45°, and they usually have channels for miter gauges. A vacuum connector allows the machine to be connected to a shop vacuum, to reduce the wood dust in the air during sanding.

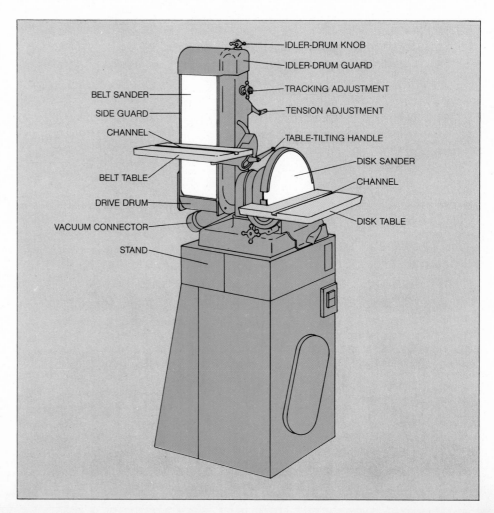

## Safety Precautions for Power Sanders

In addition to the safety rules for all power tools *(page 9)*, observe these precautions for power sanders:

□ Hold the work with your fingers on the top edge or the upper face of the stock, to avoid sanding your fingertips.

□ When sanding a small object, tack a piece of scrap wood to the back of the object, to use as a gripping block.

□ Feed the work against the rotation of a belt sander, to prevent the work from being pulled off the belt.

□ Hold the work against the downward rotation of a disk sander, to prevent the piece from being lifted off the disk.

□ Remove all wood dust before sanding metal objects; metal sanding throws sparks that might ignite the wood dust.

□ Wear goggles and a respirator while sanding, and use a vacuum attachment when doing a great deal of sanding.

□ Keep a tubular sander away from clothing; fabric can be lifted by the abrasive and wrapped around the tube.

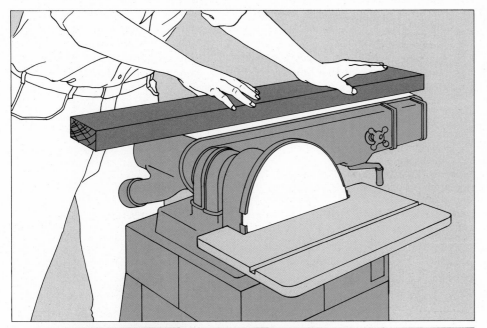

## Using a Belt and Disk to Sand Flat Surfaces

**Sanding a lengthwise surface.** Remove the idler-drum guard and the belt table, and lock the belt unit in a horizontal position. With the motor on, grip the board with your left hand and feed it onto the belt with your right hand, against the rotation of the belt. Keep the grain parallel to the belt, and move the board along the length of the belt in a continuous motion, maintaining a light, even pressure. Make repeated passes over the belt until the surface is smooth.

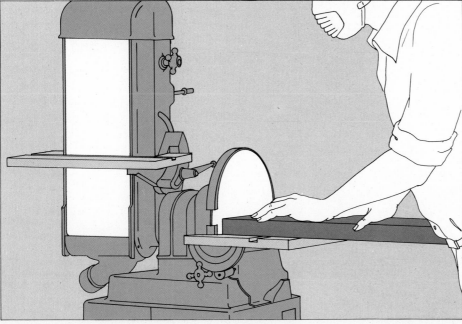

**Sanding ends.** For a square end, position the disk table horizontally, using a try square to set it perpendicular to the sanding disk. With the motor on, hold the end of the board against the left side of the disk, on the downward side of the rotation, and move it back and forth between the left edge and the center of the disk while maintaining light, continuous pressure. Use a miter gauge if necessary, to keep the wood flush against the disk.

To sand a beveled end, set the disk table at the desired angle, using a T bevel to match the angles of disk and board. Sand the bevel as you would a square end, moving it between the left edge and the center of the disk.

# Adapting the Belt Sander to Curved Surfaces

**Sanding an inside curve.** Remove the idler-drum guard, and tilt the sander until the idler drum is at a convenient working height. With the unit locked in place, turn on the motor and gently pass the inside of the curved piece over the belt at the idler drum, against the rotation of the belt. Maintain a light, even pressure and a continuous motion. At the completion of each pass, return to the starting point; repeat until you are satisfied with the finish.

**Sanding an outside curve.** With the belt unit locked in a vertical position, remove the idler-drum guard, the side guard and the back plate; then reduce the tension until the belt yields slightly when pressed. Turn on the motor and move the curved piece against the back of the belt, pressing against it slightly so that the belt follows the curve of the piece. Pay close attention to the way the loosened belt tracks over the drums, and adjust it as necessary.

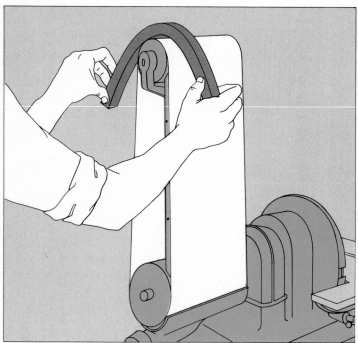

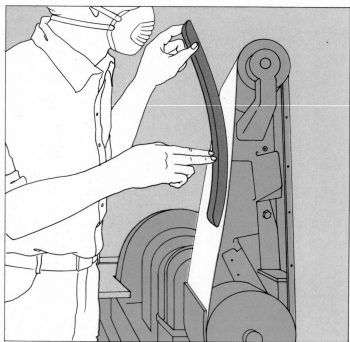

## A Template for Sanding Identical Concave Curves

**1** **Installing the template.** With the sanding belt removed from the drums, fasten a wooden template of the desired shape to the metal base plate of the belt assembly, which runs between the drums. To remove the belt, take off the idler-drum guard and the side guard and reduce the tension until the belt slips easily from the unit. Use a band saw to cut out the template, making it the width of the belt and no longer than the distance between the drums, matching the profile of the template to the inside curve of the piece being sanded.

Screw a block of scrap wood to the side of the template; then bolt the wood block to the flanged edge of the base plate, drilling holes through the wood block to match the bolt holes in the flange. Work the sanding belt back onto the drums and over the template, adjusting the tension and the tracking as necessary.

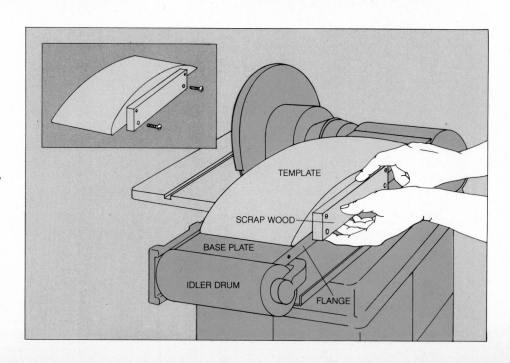

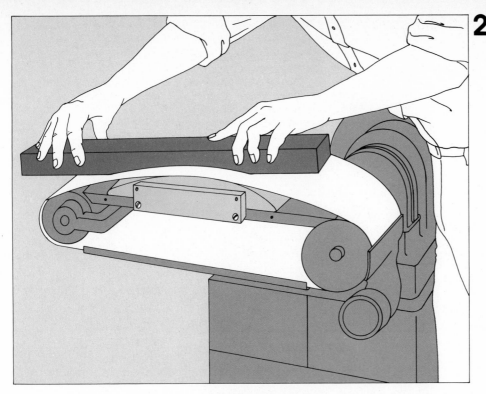

**2** **Sanding with the template.** Hold the curved piece lightly against the shaped belt, but do not move it along the belt. Lift the work frequently to check for scorching and uneven sanding. To stop scorching, reduce the pressure on the wood. If one end of the curve is being sanded too quickly, reduce pressure at that end.

## A Tubular Sander That Follows Tight Curves

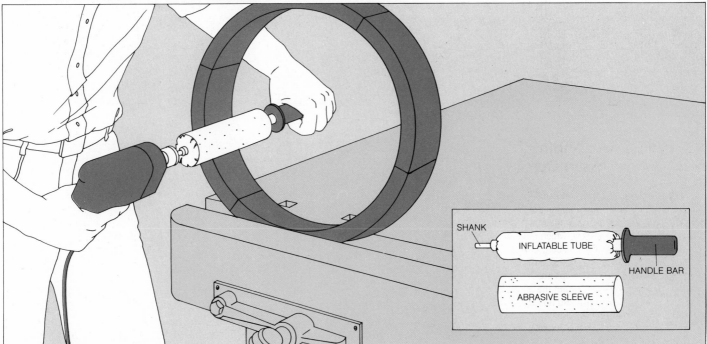

SHANK

INFLATABLE TUBE

HANDLE BAR

ABRASIVE SLEEVE

**Using a tubular sander.** Clamp the curved piece in a vise and hold the sander against its contoured surface, one hand on the power drill, the other on the handle of the sanding tube. Turn on the drill, then press the tube against the work, rolling it lightly along the curve in the direction of rotation. At the end of the curve, lift the

tube and return to the starting point; make repeated passes until the surface is smooth. If you are working in a very tight radius, roll the tube back and forth, in both directions.

To prepare the tubular sander *(inset),* slide the abrasive sleeve over the rubber cylinder and in-

flate the cylinder with a bicycle pump. Insert the sander shank in the power drill and tighten the chuck. On simple curves, use enough air pressure in the tube to hold the abrasive surface taut; for compound curves, use less air pressure, so that the abrasive surface will conform to subtle changes in the shape of the work.

# 4

# Skin-deep Beauty with Veneers

**A fretwork border for a tabletop.** Strips of border inlay set into a mahogany tabletop create in a short time a decorative effect that once took hours of deft and painstaking craftsmanship. The inlays, which come in dozens of styles—ranging from Classical Greek to American Indian—are cut with a craft knife and a straightedge, then set into a router-cut groove.

To a poet, veneer is a symbol of shallow deceit, a false front of beauty that inevitably falls away to reveal some kind of evil. To a craftsman, veneer is a thin layer of wood that turns a plain board into a beautiful one. But it also does much more. It is wood that does things no other kind of wood can do. Veneer makes plain boards stronger and more resistant to warping. It hides joints and makes them stronger, too. More important, veneer frees the craftsman to display the grain of wood in ways that are economically, structurally or physically impossible with solid lumber.

Though veneer is almost as fragile as an eggshell and is produced from wood that is soaked in boiling water to soften it before it is cut, the rotary or reciprocating machinery that makes it is anything but delicate. Rotary equipment can take the form of a giant lathe that has a single blade as wide as the log is long. The motor that spins the log is powerful enough to send the veneer, in the form of one immense shaving, pouring forth from the surface of the log at the rate of up to 400 feet per minute. A second type of rotary machine holds a half-round log against a rotating shaft. With each rotation the log is brought a little closer to the blade, and a slice of veneer is peeled off in an arc gentler than the arcs of the growth rings. Because the wood is cut on a curve, rotary equipment gives grain effects that would be impossible to achieve with flat boards. The method creates a grain pattern that magnifies the width of the rings—more so when the veneer is cut from the full log than in half-round cutting.

Reciprocating machines work something like the cold-cuts slicer in a butcher shop. The wood stock—a squared-off log called a flitch—is attached to a moving plate and driven sideways past a fixed blade that peels off a slice at a time. As the sheets come off the machine, they are numbered and stacked in order so that woodworkers can make use of the mirror-image grain patterns that once-adjacent surfaces present. Sometimes the flitch is first cut in quarters lengthwise, to yield grain patterns like those of quartersawed boards. Reciprocating machines can slice up otherwise useless parts of a tree—and with spectacular results. For instance, injured areas, too unstable for most woodworking, give an exquisite, rolling pattern called burl.

A single log flitch 8 feet long and 2 feet square can produce 30,720 square feet of veneer surface. Because the veneer-making process uses wood so efficiently, consuming virtually every part of the tree, the expensive pursuit of exotic woods becomes worthwhile. More than 200 varieties of wood are available, each one sliced up with something of the diamond cutter's sensibility, for a bountiful harvest of beauty that is at the most $1/28$ inch deep. To the woodworker, that is deep enough.

# Gluing a Thin Coat of Wood over a Solid Base

The art of veneering—layering a thin skin of decorative wood over a common wood—was once practiced only by master craftsmen. But modern glues and improved techniques for cutting veneers from raw logs have changed all that. Now a home craftsman, working with a small kit of specialized tools, can make delightful transformations in the surfaces of furniture, doors, even architectural trim. Many of the necessary tools, as well as the other materials used in veneering, can be found at local lumberyards and hardware stores, although for some items you may have to use mail-order companies that sell woodworking supplies.

Most of the veneers produced today are sliced from half-round sections of tree trunk or from squared-off logs called flitches. High-precision blades slice the wood into sheets 1/40 to 1/28 inch thick—the thickness of 10 to 20 pages of notepaper. The sheets are stacked flat in the same sequence in which they are sliced, their edges are generally left untrimmed and they are priced by the square foot. In another form, the veneer is sliced much thinner, only 1/64 inch thick, and glued to a paper backing. This flexible veneer is sold in 8-foot rolls, 18 to 36 inches wide, and in narrow strips for edging.

In addition to taking veneers from the tree trunk, manufacturers also make use of parts of the tree normally considered waste wood—the roots, burls, stumps and crotches that are too unstable for construction. These waste woods yield veneers with exotic grain patterns and colorings, from the whirling spirals of burls to the V-shaped grain of crotch wood—taken from a section where a major limb branches from the trunk.

So distinctive are some of these grain patterns that the tree species is instantly recognizable. Walnut, elm and maple, for example, are notable for their flamboyant burl and stump-wood patterns, rosewood and zebrawood for their varicolored stripes, oak and mahogany for their rippling grain. Matched sections of these patterned veneers can produce designs that seem almost three-dimensional.

Applying veneer can be done in several ways, but the process always begins with a flattening procedure. With highly patterned woods, which tend to be brittle and wavy, this step is essential. To flatten such veneer, each sheet is dampened with a sponge until it is saturated but not sodden. Then the sheet is pressed between two pieces of plywood; clamps are used to increase the pressure gradually as the veneer dries. When the wood is only slightly clammy to the touch, it is ready to use. Flexible veneer rolls can be pressed flat without having to be dampened first.

For large surfaces, such as doors and tabletops, the best way to apply veneer is to glue and clamp it to the base. Usually the veneer is applied in sections, and adjacent sections must be perfectly spliced, so that the gap between them is almost indiscernible. To make such a joint, the joining edges are trimmed either with a utility knife or with a special veneer saw, which makes a thin, straight cut.

Veneer pins are used to hold the sections of veneer in place temporarily; these pins have needle-like points that leave nearly invisible holes. Later, when the sections are glued down, gummed paper tape holds the spliced edges together until the glue dries. This tape, which has a water-soluble backing, is preferable to masking tape, which might lift veneer slivers when it is removed.

Clamping, which ensures a tight bond between the veneer and the base, is also an important step in veneering. The pressure exerted by clamping should bear down directly and evenly on the surface beneath. This kind of clamping is best done with a caul—a piece of particleboard or plywood with 2-by-4 cross braces clamped over it to distribute the pressure. For a surface less than 2 feet across, use heavy weights instead of cross braces and clamps, and distribute the weights evenly.

On curved surfaces, such as those on rounded cabinet fronts, it is almost impossible to achieve uniform pressure by clamping. For such jobs the preferred method of pressing the veneer against the base is a technique called hammer veneering, which uses no clamps at all. Instead, the veneer is systematically pressed smooth against the glued surface with a spade-shaped tool called a veneer hammer. Traditionally, hammer veneering relied on hide glue, which had to be heated, and hard-earned skill; but today yellow glue simplifies the job and produces good results.

A third veneering method uses contact cement, which bonds instantly and also requires no clamping. But instant bonding creates problems because it allows no corrections. Contact cement is best reserved for veneering small areas, such as the edges of tables and shelves. It also is easiest to use with flexible veneers, which flatten with light pressure and can be cut with utility scissors.

Regardless of the method used, to be successful, veneering must be carefully planned. The base should be a stable wood, such as pine, mahogany or poplar. Splinters should be smoothed away and holes filled with wood putty.

If you are working with stock less than 1/2 inch thick, prepare to veneer both surfaces—otherwise the piece will warp. And keep in mind that the grain of veneer should run parallel to the grain of solid wood but perpendicular to the grain of plywood.

As you work, keep your tools close at hand so that you do not have to hunt for them just as the glue is freshly spread. And be prepared for repairs—but do not attempt to make them until the glue dries. Highly figured veneers may need patching, cracks may develop along the grain, and sections of veneer may even lift and need to be reglued and reclamped. When the job is complete, finish the veneer just as you would solid wood, with penetrating oil or varnish.

## Pair-bonded Veneers

**Combining veneers for effect.** Consecutive sheets of veneer cut from a flitch are nearly identical in pattern but can be arranged to create completely dissimilar designs. Two sheets, opened as if they were pages of a book, present a mirror image and are called book-matched veneer; you can extend book-matching over large surfaces by flipping over every second sheet. Sheets laid just as they come from the stack, in a repeating pattern, are called slip-matched; this pattern is most effective with long narrow sheets cut from narrow flitches.

Veneers with very straight grain lend themselves well to a diamond arrangement, or to a variation in which the diamond shape is reversed so that the grain of the wood radiates from a central point. For either of these patterns, start by cutting four identical rectangles of veneer, with the grain running diagonally across each of the rectangles. Then position the rectangles edge to edge, forming either a pattern of concentric diamonds or a pattern of radiating lines.

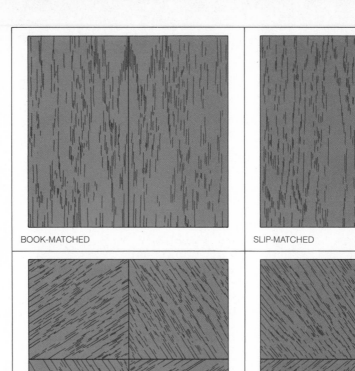

BOOK-MATCHED

SLIP-MATCHED

DIAMOND

REVERSE DIAMOND

---

## Virtues and Failings of Veneering Glues

☐ WHITE GLUE is an inexpensive, water-soluble adhesive that takes 4 to 6 hours to harden. This slow set-up time is an advantage in veneering large areas, because it allows alignments to be perfected before the new surface is locked in place. White glue does require extensive clamping, however, and once the job is done, the veneer must be protected from moisture or it will lift from its base. Apply white glue with a paint roller, a brush or a comb-type glue spreader. When using white glue with highly figured veneers, which warp when exposed to water, spread glue only on the base. Clean tools in warm water.

☐ YELLOW GLUE, also known as aliphatic resin or carpenter's glue, is more water-resistant than white glue. It sets up in 30 minutes and requires swifter clamping. It is the best of the modern glues for hammer veneering. Use a paint roller to spread the glue on both the base and the back of the veneer. Let the glue rest for five minutes, until it is tacky, before pressing the veneer to the base. Yellow glue takes overnight to dry completely, but tools should be cleaned immediately in water.

☐ CONTACT CEMENT is sometimes labeled "veneer glue." It bonds instantly and thus needs no clamping, but it does not allow corrections once the veneer is positioned. Use a paintbrush to spread the cement on both the veneer and the base. Let it dry 5 to 15 minutes, or until it is no longer sticky. Then carefully press the veneer in place with your fingers and a roller. Use lacquer thinner to remove drips and to clean your tools.

☐ HIDE GLUE, which is made from the hide and hooves of animals, has been the classic glue for veneering for centuries. It is sold as a powder to be mixed with water. The advantage of hide glue is that it dries at room temperature to make a durable bond but softens under heat, simplifying minor adjustments and repairs. But it must be heated during use and kept within the narrow range of 130° to 150° F. Today most woodworkers avoid the inconvenience of a heated gluepot and heated metal tools, and opt for a more modern glue.

☐ IRON-ON GLUE SHEETS are paper coated on both sides with hot-melt glue. The sheets are placed between the base and the veneer, then pressed with a household iron set at LOW. They can be cut to shape with scissors. They are quick and convenient for small areas, but they produce a less durable bond than the more conventional glues.

# Splicing and Clamping Large Veneer Surfaces

**1 Splicing adjoining sheets.** Arrange sheets of veneer in the desired grain pattern, with their joining edges overlapped by ½ inch and their outside edges protruding ¼ inch beyond the edges of the base. Clamp a straightedge along the line to be spliced and, using a utility knife, cut through both sheets at once. Slice in short strokes along the guide, to prevent the thin blade from following the curve of the grain.

To make a splicing cut with a veneer saw *(inset)*, place the tapered edge of the blade against the straightedge, and pull the blade along the seam line, again cutting with short, smooth strokes in one direction only. For very thick veneer, place the flat edge of the blade against the straightedge, and saw back and forth; proceed carefully, to avoid splintering the surface.

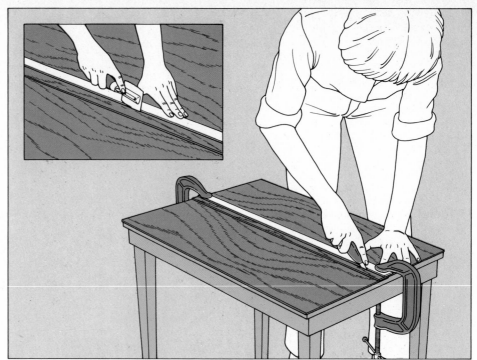

**2 Spreading the glue.** To coat both veneer and base with glue, lay the veneer face down on a work surface covered with newspaper; use a small paint roller to spread glue thickly and evenly to the edges. To prevent the veneer from shifting and excess glue from smearing its face, hold the sheets steady with an awl or an old screwdriver. Roll glue onto the base in the same manner, wiping any drips with a rag.

Lay the veneer on the base, matching the grain patterns along the seam line and maintaining an even ¼-inch overlap at the edges of the base. Press and smooth the surface with your hands, shifting the veneer sections slightly to close any gaps in the seam. Then secure the sheets with veneer pins spaced 6 inches apart and about 3 inches from the seam line.

**3 Rolling the veneer.** Use a wallpaper-seam roller to press out air pockets and excess glue from between the veneer and the base. Push the roller from the center of the base toward its edges, wiping off the extruded glue as you go. Roll along the seam to press it flat.

Secure the spliced edges by covering the seam with paper tape. Cut a piece of tape the same length as the seam and dampen it with a sponge, then smooth it in place along the seam. At 12-inch intervals, fasten additional 4-inch strips of tape across the seam. Remove the pins.

VENEER PINS

**4** **Clamping the work.** To apply uniform pressure to the veneered surface, cover it with a caul held in place by clamped cross braces. Cut the caul from plywood or particleboard, making it large enough to protrude ½ inch beyond the edges of the veneered surface. To prevent the caul from becoming glued to the veneer when pressure is applied, cover the veneer with wax paper. Then lift the caul gently onto the veneer; take care not to shift the veneer, because the glue will still be soft.

Position 2-by-4 cross braces on edge across the caul at 16-inch intervals, slipping a scrap piece of veneer beneath the center of each 2-by-4 to increase the pressure at the center of the caul. Tighten clamps on the center cross brace first, so that glue will be forced from the center of the caul toward its edges. Wipe off any excess glue, and continue tightening the cross brace until no more glue appears. Then tighten clamps on the end cross braces.

Let the glue dry 12 hours. Remove the clamps, lift off the caul and peel off the wax paper.

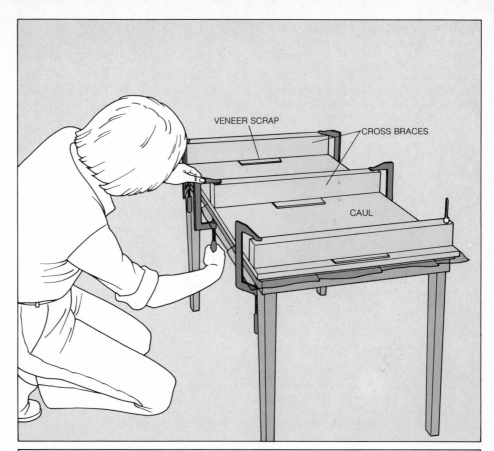

VENEER SCRAP

CROSS BRACES

CAUL

**5** **Trimming the edges.** Using the caul to protect your worktable, turn the veneered surface upside down and trim off the protruding veneer with a veneer saw. Start at a corner and cut along the edge to within a few inches of the next corner. Then turn the blade and cut in the opposite direction, to keep from tearing off the fragile corners of the veneer.

When all of the edges have been trimmed, set the veneered surface right side up; dampen the paper tape with a sponge, then remove it. Sand away any residual glue or tape.

# A Time-honored Method for Veneering over Curves

**Two veneer hammers.** Both the professional's veneer hammer *(left)* and the homemade veneer hammer *(right)* have smooth metal blades designed to press veneer against a curved base. The store-bought version has a hardwood handle with a spade-shaped metal head, 3½ inches wide; the upper end of the head is used as a grip, for bearing down on the veneer. The simple and inexpensive homemade veneer hammer works like a squeegee. The handle is a ¾-inch dowel, 11 inches long, filed down at one end; it fits into a socket drilled at the center of the hardwood head. The two parts are secured with glue and a 1-inch screw. The head, which is cut from ½-inch stock, is 3½ inches long by 2½ inches wide. The blade is made of ¼-inch-thick brass or aluminum plate, set to protrude ¼ inch beyond the bottom edge of the head. Its working edge is filed smooth and its corners are rounded, to keep them from gouging or scratching the veneer. Matching holes are drilled through the plate and the head, and the two are fastened together with bolts and wing nuts, making the plate detachable for cleaning. Caution: Do not use iron or steel for the plate. Either could react with the tannic acid present in most woods and leave stains on the veneer surface.

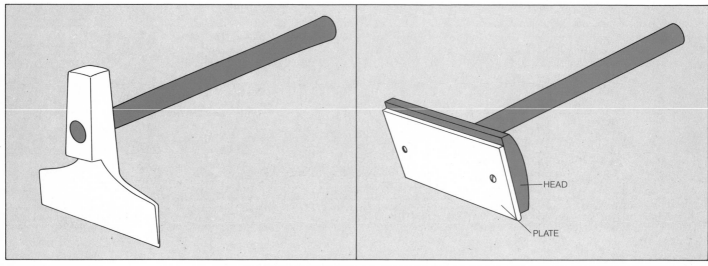

HEAD
PLATE

**Using the veneer hammer.** After laying the glued veneer against the base, smooth it with a hammer, forcing out any excess glue and flattening any air pockets. Then bear down with considerable weight, pressing against the head of the hammer, and stroke repeatedly along the veneer in the direction of the grain. Do not work across the grain; this might separate the glue-soaked wood fibers, causing the veneer to crack as it dries.

When using a veneer hammer on spliced veneers, tape the sections together before you glue them on. Work over the taped veneers as if they were a single continuous sheet. Take off the tape only after the glue has dried overnight.

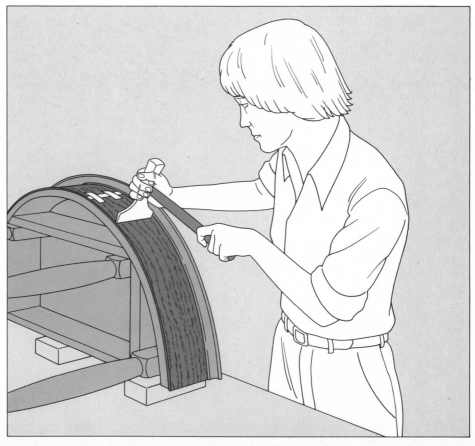

## Deflating an Air Pocket

**1** **Piercing the veneer.** If an air pocket develops after the glue has hardened, determine its dimensions by tapping on the surface with a fingernail; it will make a dry, hollow sound. Make an X-shaped incision at the center of the pocket with a craft knife and a metal rule, cutting diagonally across the grain. Lift the flaps of veneer with a palette knife, then use the craft knife to gently scrape away the old glue from the veneer and the base beneath; blow out the dried glue particles. If the flaps are too stiff to bend easily, dampen them with a sponge.

Insert fresh yellow glue underneath the flaps, using either a glue injector or a small artist's brush. Then roll the veneer flat and wipe away the excess glue as in Step 3, page 122.

**2** **Pressing the repair.** To shorten the glue's drying time and keep flaps of veneer from lifting, press the repaired area with a household iron set at LOW (150° to 170° F.). First cover the repaired area with a piece of wax paper, to prevent sticking, and a folded dish towel, to protect the veneer from scorching. Then press the iron against the area for 30 seconds; check to see if the glue is holding down the flaps, and repeat as necessary until the glue is hard. Sand the repair lightly, following the grain of the veneer.

## Grafting a Matching Patch

**Shaping the patch.** Cut away the splintered edges of a veneer split, leaving a clean outline; then make a pattern of the damaged area by placing a piece of paper over the outline and rubbing it with a blunt pencil. Use the pattern to cut a patch from veneer that matches as closely as possible the grain and color of the veneer surrounding the split. Spread the patch with yellow glue, insert it in the split, and roll it flat. Wipe away the excess glue, and press the patch with a warm iron as in Step 2, above.

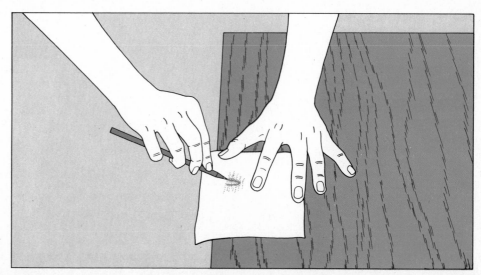

## Splicing a Decorative Band onto a Veneered Surface

**1** **Slicing the banding seams.** Lap the banding veneer over one edge of the veneered surface, allowing it to overhang that surface slightly. Clamp a straightedge along what will be the seam line between the two pieces of veneer, and slice through both layers at once. Repeat along the other edges of the veneered surface, numbering and marking each banding piece to record its position and seam line. Position the banding along each edge in such a way that its grain runs either parallel or perpendicular to the edge of the veneered surface.

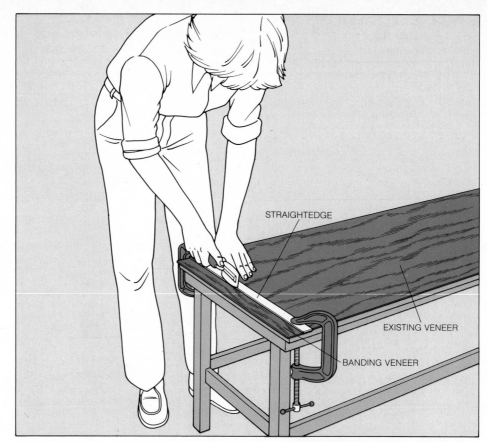

STRAIGHTEDGE

EXISTING VENEER

BANDING VENEER

**2** **Removing the existing veneer.** Clamp the straightedge along the seam line of the veneered surface, and pry off the edge of the veneer with a chisel, held bevel down. Press down on the straightedge as you work, to avoid damaging the veneer inside the seam line. If the edge of the veneer does crack, repair it before proceeding. Remove the veneer from the other edges in the same way, and scrape the dried glue from the cleared areas.

Using paper tape that has water-soluble gum, fasten the pieces of banding in place, matching the seam lines and overlapping the ends of the banding at each corner. Trim the overlapping ends into neatly spliced miters, using either a chisel (*inset*) or a craft knife and a straightedge. When all the pieces have been cut to fit, dampen the paper tape and remove it.

With an inexpensive paintbrush, spread an even coating of contact cement on the back of a banding piece and on the cleared edges. When the contact cement has cured, lay overlapping strips of wax paper, about 6 inches wide, over the cement-covered edge.

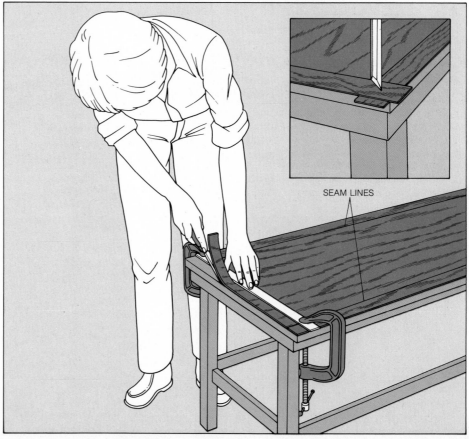

SEAM LINES

**3** **Setting the banding.** Lay the banding over the wax paper and, starting at a corner, slowly pull away the strips of wax paper one at a time, each time pressing the veneer against the exposed edge. Then flatten the banding with a roller. Install the other banding sections in the same way, being especially careful to fit the mitered ends together precisely.

**4** **Trimming the banding.** Using a block plane with its blade set for a very shallow cut, shave away the overlapping edges of banding. Hold the plane with its sole flush to the edge and slide it forward with short strokes, to avoid pulling away chips of veneer. Plane until the veneer is flush with the edge of the veneered surface.

## Applying Veneer Edging

**Rolling the edgings on.** To veneer a vertical edge, cut strips of flexible veneer to size or buy edging tape in the appropriate width, and apply it with contact cement and a roller. If you cut your own edging, align the grain to run lengthwise along the side. Lay on the cement in a thin coat, so that the line where the edging veneer meets the surface veneer will be less noticeable.

When the cement spread on the two adjoining surfaces has cured, start at one corner and position the edging with one hand as you press it smooth with the roller. If necessary, trim the edging at the next corner for a precise fit, before attaching edging to the adjoining side.

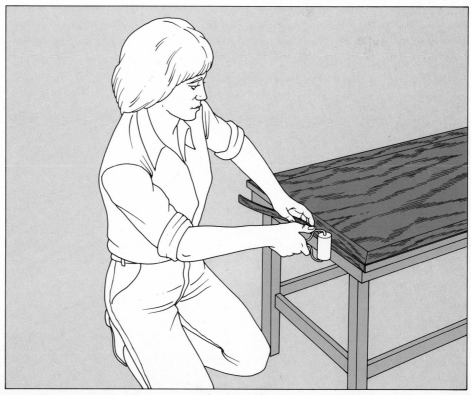

# Highlighting a Surface with Inlaid Designs

Usually applied over the entire surface of a less attractive base, veneer can also be set into a recess cut into the surface. This technique, called inlaying, is used to highlight a beautifully grained piece of wood or to make an ordinary one more interesting. And though natural or colored wood veneers are the most common material for inlays, leather, ivory and mother-of-pearl are often used as well.

Inlays take many forms. The most elaborate probably is marquetry, which is made up of small chips, often of different colors and irregular shapes, assembled like a mosaic to form a symbol or a picture. Another form, parquetry, uses small, straight-edged chips to form geometric patterns. Border strips are a form that combines long straight pieces with tiny chips to make narrow ribbon-like patterns. All of these intricate designs are usually assembled first, then inlaid as a unit into a recess cut exactly to fit. Designs made of larger pieces of veneer may be assembled directly in the recess, however, using the same technique as that used to cut and fit adjoining veneer sheets *(page 122)*.

The crucial first step in inlaying is making the recess, which must have a consistent depth and must match the outline of the insert exactly. When you are working on solid wood, a power router is an excellent tool for the first part of this job—removing the bulk of the waste from the recess. You will also need a chisel for squaring corners and, on designs with intricate outlines, a craft knife for cutting around the perimeter and some chisels and gouges for clearing the waste from crevices. When you cut a recess into a veneered surface, you first cut the perimeter with a craft knife, then remove the waste with a chisel *(page 126)*.

Although you can make inlay inserts yourself, a variety of ready-made patterns of many sizes and shapes are available from woodworking suppliers. These inserts are usually shipped with a piece of brown paper glued to the finish face and with the insert set into a piece of scrap veneer to protect its edges. Carefully cut away this excess veneer before inlaying the insert, but leave the brown paper in place until after the insert is glued down; sand the paper off during the finishing.

Most inserts are supplied in thicknesses ranging from $\frac{1}{28}$ inch to $\frac{1}{14}$ inch. Border strips are available in 3-foot lengths and in widths ranging from about $\frac{1}{16}$ inch to 1¼ inches. Because supposedly identical border designs may vary slightly from lot to lot, it is best to order a few extra strips for each project so that if you need to patch or correct previous work, you can match it exactly.

If you decide to make your own inlays, you can add variety by coloring or shading the veneer you use. Colorfast fabric dyes, mixed with one quarter the water called for in the instructions, are good for tinting veneers of such light-colored, absorbent woods as poplar or holly. By dipping only the edge of the veneer into the dye, you can obtain a color gradation with the darkest tone at the edge, where the veneer touches the dye. You can also use ink to color veneer, either by soaking or by applying it with a pen or a brush.

To shade the natural wood on the edge of any kind of veneer—to get a three-dimensional effect—dip the edge into a tray of fine sand, heated over a stove or a burner. The scorching of the veneer will be darkest at the point dipped deepest into the sand. In using coloring or shading techniques, always make the veneer a little darker than the final color or shade desired, since finish sanding will remove the darkest surface layer.

## Using Strips of Inlay to Form a Border

**1** **Routing a straight groove.** Outline the groove needed for the inlay, and fit a router with a bit appropriate to the groove's width. Measure the distance from the perimeter of the bit to the edge of the router base, and then clamp a straight-edged board this distance from the inner edge of the groove outline. Set the bit to a cutting depth just less than the thickness of the inlay. Butt the router base against the board, turn on the router, and lower it to the surface of the work. Rout from left to right. Take care not to rout beyond the ends of the outline. When you finish the cut, turn the router off and wait for the bit to stop spinning before you lift it.

If the groove outline is wider than the router bit, reposition the straight-edged board as often as needed until all unrouted stock between the groove outlines is removed. When such a groove turns a corner, finish all passes on one side before proceeding to the adjacent side.

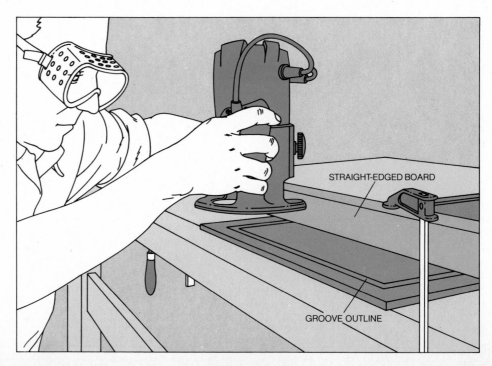

STRAIGHT-EDGED BOARD

GROOVE OUTLINE

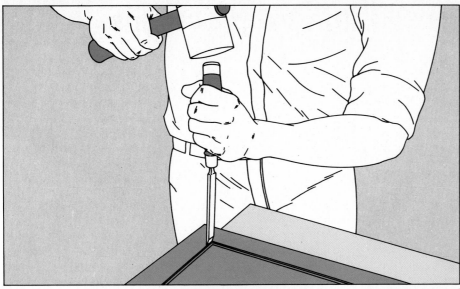

**2 Squaring corners of a routed groove.** Position a sharp, wide wood chisel over the uncut area at the outer corner of the groove, aligning the flat side of the blade with the edge of the groove. Tap the chisel lightly with a mallet. Make an identical cut on the other side of the outer corner. Then use the chisel to undercut the waste in the corner. Clean any splinters from the edge of the groove with a craft knife.

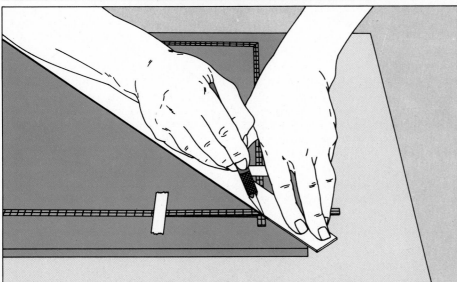

**3 Fitting the inlay in the groove.** Lay the inlay border strips in the grooves so that the patterns match where the strips overlap at the corners. Secure each strip, about 2 inches from each corner, with paper tape that has water-soluble gum. Then lay a metal straightedge diagonally across the corner; use a craft knife to cut a 45° miter through both pieces of inlay, starting at the outside corner and working in.

If the grooves are too long for a single inlay strip, lay as many strips in each groove as necessary. Allow about an inch of overlap between strips, matching the patterns at the overlap; try to arrange the overlaps so that they occur at regular intervals. Match the corner patterns as well, securing and mitering them as above. Then use the straightedge and the craft knife to cut through the overlaps along the groove, cutting across the strips at a 90° angle.

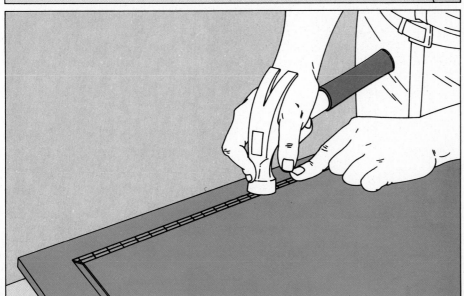

**4 Gluing the border strips.** Spread a thin coat of yellow glue on the back of each inlay strip, and then return the strips to their grooves. Use the smooth face of a hammer to press the strips firmly into the grooves, making sure that each one is properly aligned before pressing it into place. Wipe away any excess glue with a damp cloth. Cover all of the glued inlay with wax paper; then lay a piece of hardboard, plywood or particleboard over the entire surface, and weight it down with bricks or other heavy objects.

# Cutting a Recess for a Small Medallion

**1 Laying out the area.** Place the inlay in the desired position on the surface of the work. With a straightedge and a pencil, draw perpendicular lines across the inlay and the surrounding surface. Keeping the marks aligned, trace the outline of the inlay onto the work, using a scratch awl.

**2 Freehand cutting with a router.** Put a straight bit in the router, and adjust the bit depth to slightly less than the thickness of the inlay. Start the router, and lower the bit onto the surface of the work, near the center of the area to be recessed. Move the router clockwise over the area in a circular motion, taking out the waste to within $1/16$ inch of the scribed outline.

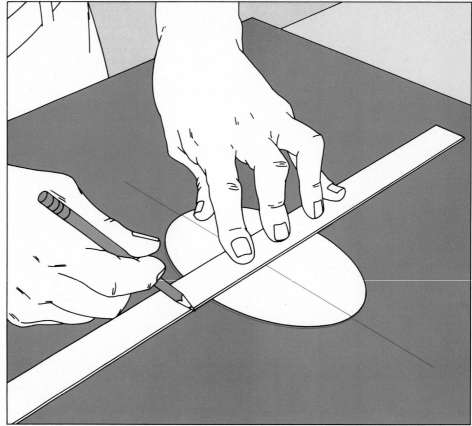

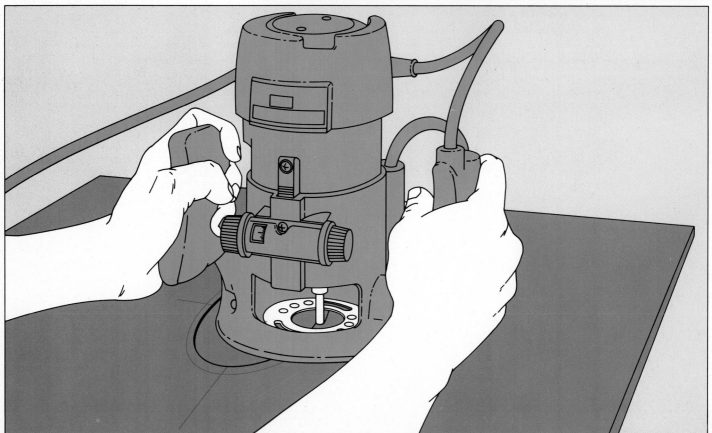

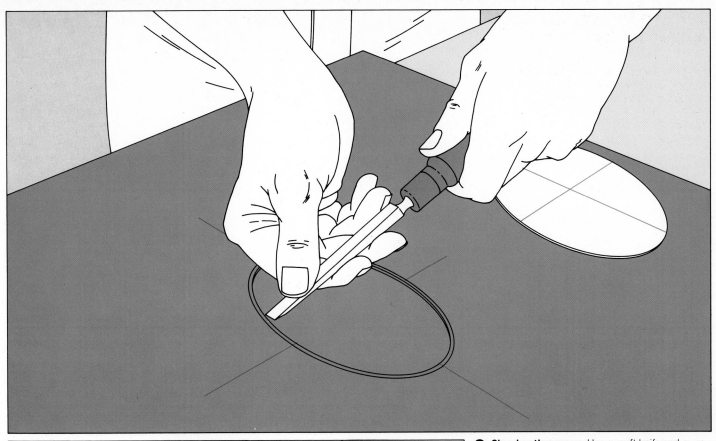

**3** **Cleaning the recess.** Use a craft knife and a chisel to clean away the waste from the edge of the recess. First deepen the scribed outline with the craft knife; then use the chisel to undercut and remove the waste. Hold the chisel, bevel edge down, in such a way that the bottom of the recess will be level.

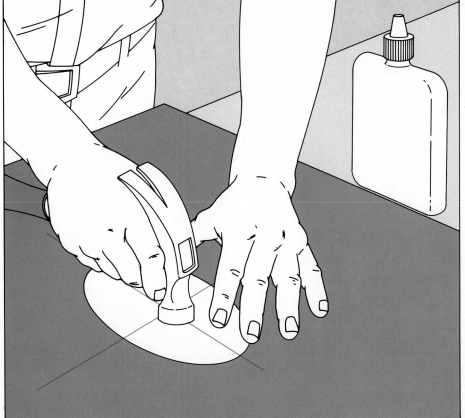

**4** **Attaching the inlay.** Spread a thin coat of yellow glue over the recessed area, and carefully lower the inlay into the recess, brown paper facing up. Match up the alignment marks, then rub the face of a hammer over the inlay, working from the center outward in a circular motion, to force out the excess glue. Secure the inlay edges temporarily with small pieces of paper tape.

**5** **Clamping the insert.** Cover the inlay with a sheet of wax paper, to prevent excess glue from sticking to the clamp assembly; then cover the inlaid area with a piece of ¼-inch plywood or hardboard slightly larger than the area of the inlay. Place a 2-by-4 on edge across the center of the plywood, and clamp the ends of the 2-by-4 to the edge of the work surface.

## Routing Out a Large Area for a Sizable Inlay

**1** **Setting up the router pattern.** For inlays that cover large areas, use a router fitted with the widest straight bit available, set to a cutting depth just slightly less than the thickness of the inlay. To make the first pass with the router, cut a groove along one edge of the area to be recessed, about $1/16$ inch in from scribed outline. Make additional passes until the groove is approximately 1½ inches wide.

Start a second groove parallel to the first and about 1½ inches away from it, again making repeated passes until the groove is 1½ inches wide. Continue cutting similar parallel grooves across the entire recess, always stopping roughly $1/16$ inch from the scribed outline.

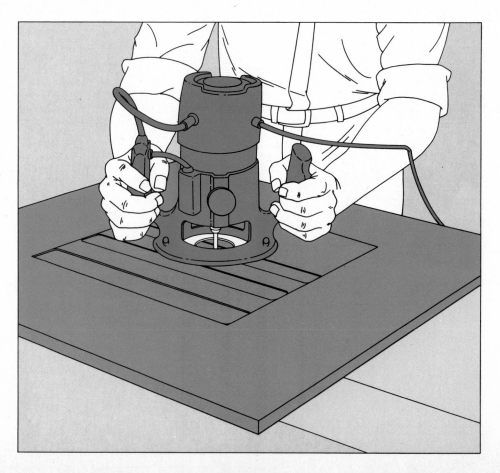

**2** **Completing the router cuts.** Again starting $\frac{1}{16}$ inch in from the edge of the recessed area, cut a second series of 1½-inch-wide parallel grooves, perpendicular to the first. Then gradually widen these grooves by making repeated passes with the router until the projections remaining are only ¼ inch to ⅜ inch wide; they will support the base of the router.

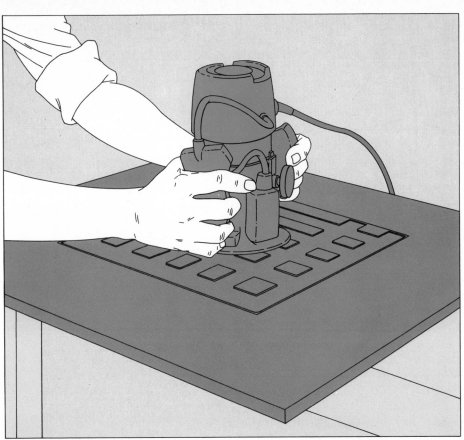

**3** **Removing the remaining scrap.** Using a sharp chisel held bevel edge down, knock away the small projections left by routing. Then remove the waste from the edge of the recessed area as shown in Step 3, page 131. Glue and set the inlay as described in Steps 2 and 3, page 122. Clamp the inlay, using the method shown in Step 4, page 123, for clamping large areas.

## Picture Credits

*The sources for the illustrations in this book are shown below. The drawings were created by Jack Arthur, Roger Essley, Charles Forsythe, John Jones, Dick Lee, John Martinez and Joan McGurren. Credits for the illustrations from left to right are separated by semicolons, from top to bottom by dashes.*

Cover: Fil Hunter. 6: Fil Hunter. 9-13: Terry Atkinson from Arts & Words. 14-19: John Massey. 20-23: Frederic F. Bigio from B-C Graphics. 24-27: Walter Hilmers Jr. from HJ Commercial Art. 28-31: William J. Hennessy Jr. 33: © 1980 Stephen Green- Armytage, courtesy George Nakashima, artist. 34: Ezra Stoller © ESTO, courtesy George Nakashima, artist. 35: Al Freni, London-Marquis, designers, courtesy L.C.S., Inc.—courtesy Howard Werner, artist. 36: Mark Sexton, courtesy Seth Stem, artist—Al Freni, Michael Coffey, artist, courtesy Westlake Gallery, Ltd. 37: G. Magnin, Eugène Vallin, artist, courtesy Musée de l'Ecole de Nancy, France. 38: Peter Ralston, Wendell Castle, artist, courtesy Mr. & Mrs. C. J. Frederick— Adam Avila, courtesy Chris Schambacher, artist. 39: Norman McGrath, Pedro Friedeberg, artist, courtesy Arnold Scaasi. 40: J. Guillot, Connaissance des Arts, François Rupert Carabin, artist, private collection, Paris. 41: Fred Holz. 42: Fil Hunter. 44-53: Frederic F. Bigio from B-C Graphics. 54-59: Gerry Gallagher. 60-65: William J. Hennessy Jr. 66-73: John Massey. 74-79: Walter Hilmers Jr. from HJ Commercial Art. 80-83: Snowden Associates, Inc. 84: Fil Hunter. 86-93: Eduino J. Pereira from Arts & Words. 94-99: Elsie J. Hennig. 100-109: Frederic F. Bigio from B-C Graphics. 110-113: John Massey. 114-117: Elsie J. Hennig. 118: Fil Hunter. 121-127: Frederic F. Bigio from B-C Graphics. 128-133: William J. Hennessy Jr.

## Acknowledgments

The index/glossary for this book was prepared by Louise Hedberg. The editors also wish to thank the following: Henry Barrow, The Woodworks, Glen Echo, Md.; Juan Bassegoda, President, Amigos de Gaudi, Barcelona, Spain; Bob Blankenship, Moisture Register Company, North Hollywood, Calif.; Emmett Bright, Rome, Italy; Mario Ceroli, Rome, Italy; Françoise Charpentier, Curator, Musée de L'Ecole de Nancy, Nancy, France; Ted Chase, Concord, Calif.; Raylene Decatur, Renwick Gallery, Washington, D.C.; Clyde Dorsett, The Pond Gallery, Alexandria, Va.; Fendrick Gallery, Washington, D.C.; Allan Fitchett, Albert Constantine & Son, Inc., New York, N.Y.; Full Circle, Alexandria, Va.; Douglas N. Heyman, Fries Beall & Sharp Co., Springfield, Va.; John Kelsey, Editor, *Fine Woodworking* magazine, Newtown, Conn.; Peter Kramer, Washington, Va.; Johannes Krogull, Melle, West Germany; Andrejs Legzdins, Stockholm, Sweden; Mike Mangan, Ken Page, Sears, Roebuck & Co., Chicago, Ill.; John Ott, June Sprigg, Hancock Shaker Village Museum, Pittsfield, Mass.; Robert Petersen, Robert Petersen Associates, Alexandria, Va.; Joanne Polster, American Craft Library, The American Craft Council, New York, N.Y.; Patricia Ridgeway, Seraph, Washington, D.C.; Giuseppe Rivadossi, Brescia, Italy; Jerry Siegel, Jenks and Sons, Inc., Washington, D.C.; Ole Thrane, L.C.S. Inc., New York, N.Y.; Todd M. Volpe, Jordan-Volpe Gallery, New York, N.Y.; Bill Welcome, Wendell Castle Inc., Scottsdale, N.Y. The editors would also like to express their appreciation to Edgar Henry and Wendy Murphy, writers, for their assistance with the preparation of this volume.

# Index/Glossary

Printed in U.S.A.